What Is Right with the World:
The Human Urge for Peace

What Is Right with the World: The Human Urge for Peace

Swami Veda Bharati, D. Litt.

AHYMSA PUBLISHERS

Editor: Ron Valle, Ph.D.

Cover and book design: David Spohn

Copyright © 2010 Swami Veda Bharati

2nd Edition 2013

ISBN 978-0-9835992-8-9

Ahymsa Publishers
631 University Ave. N.E.
Minneapolis, MN 55413
info@ahymsapublishers.com

Distributed by Lotus Press, PO Box 325, Twin Lakes, WI 53181 U.S.A.,
www.lotuspress.com, 800-824-6396, lotuspress@lotuspress.com

Printed in the USA

BIOGRAPHY

Swami Veda Bharati has researched the process of peace since early childhood. Born into a Sanskrit-speaking family in India, he has traveled and taught the methods of yoga and meditation from his early youth for over 63 years. Having made a study of how individual and societal conflicts have been resolved in ancient civilizations and modern cultures, he has helped many thousands realize peace, both as individuals and within their societies.

Holding a doctoral degree from a Western university, Swami Veda has written many books on Indian spirituality, and has established Yoga and meditation centers in Africa, Europe, and the Americas that he guides from his ashram in the foothills of the Himalayas.

He has lectured at universities across the globe, as well as at the World Parliament of Religions in both Cape Town, South Africa and Barcelona, Spain; Shakespeare's Globe Theatre in London, England; the Episcopal Cathedral in Salt Lake City, Utah; and the UNESCO Centre for Peace Studies in Innsbruck, Austria. He has also been honored at Palacio Vecchio in Firenze, Italy. He was part of a dialogue with Taoist leaders at the Chinese Taoist Association headquarters in Beijing, China, and has been active in the interfaith dialogues organized by the Global Peace Initiative of Women (GPIW), through which he has established close relationships with eminent Sufi leaders.

He continues to guide his followers on the paths of inner peace and societal harmony. More information is available at www.swamiveda.org.

ALSO BY SWAMI VEDA BHARATI:

Superconscious Meditation
Meditation — The Art & Science
Meditation And The Art Of Dying
God
Mantra And Meditation
Mantras — The Sacred Chants
The Song Of Silence — Subtleties In Sadhana
Philosophy Of Hatha Yoga
Yoga Sutras Of Patanjali, Volumes 1 & 2
Introducing Mahabharata Bhishma
Subtler Than The Subtle — The Upanishad Of The White Horse
Wanam — Africa And India
Saying Nothing Says It All — Sayings
Night Birds — A Collection Of Short Writings
The Light Of Ten Thousand Suns
108 Blossoms From The Guru Granth Garden
Yogi In The Lab

TABLE OF CONTENTS

DEDICATION

To all women and men of wisdom to whom we owe a debt of gratitude for what is right with the world. They who from diverse cultures of sanctity are interpreting ancient traditions, sacrificing themselves for the preservation of this heritage, and tirelessly gifting it to guide present world cultures toward a benign future.

ACKNOWLEDGMENTS

With gratitude I wish to acknowledge the contribution of those who invited me to various conferences to make the presentations that have now become chapters in this book.

With regard to the first edition that was printed by the Ahymsin Publishers in Rishikesh, Imdia: Deepest gratitude goes to Lalita Arya, our co-ordinating editor, Sharada Bhajan, Bhola Shankar Dabral, in charge of printing and publishing, Dr. Dowlat Budhram, Winston Ho-Yow, Lakshmi Lall, Stomya Persaud, and Krita Sawh for having made untiring efforts to help produce this work.

Thanks to Cristina Nobile and Debora Ghiraldelli for help with the pictures in Florence, to Angiras Arya for the photo of the beautiful oil painting of Jesus, gifted to him by students and friends from Ukraine. We are also grateful to Mr. Madhav Kamat for researching the lovely image of Mother Mary, to Jared Hertzburg for the use of his Peace Poster, to Shalini Persaud for the Peace Sign, and to all the photographers.

Thanks to Dianella Melani, whose poignant water color painting appeared on the front cover of the first edition that was printed in India. It represents humanity's collective pilgrimage to a summit. The original painting was a gift to the author. Thanks to Juan Burwell for the cover design for that edition.

For the current edition: My sincerest appreciation for the diligent editing by Dr. Ron Valle; David Spohn for the book and cover design; Carolyn Kott Washburne for careful proofreading and, above all , for all the volunteers leaders of Ahymsa Publishers, namely, Wesley van Linda, Carol Weiler and Michael Smith.

Thanks also to all those whose names are too numerous to mention, who have helped with this book.

May all who help others be helped a million fold.

MESSAGE FROM CLAES NOBEL

With great interest I read your book the very night I received it. I found your various proposals and self-evident steps for the advancement of Peace to be thought-provoking, doable, and much needed in the world of today that reflects so much confusion and perplexity. *What Is Right With The World: The Human Urge For Peace* should be a mandatory guide and handbook for every political and religious person, whether leaders or laypersons.

I did this priority reading because the elusive ideal of peace is one of my foremost interests. And I fully agree with my great-granduncle Alfred Nobel when he said "War is the horror of horrors and the crime of crimes." Consequently, I am in the process of seeking to advance world wide *Universal Peace,* which concept stands for much more than the mere absence of war. It represents the totality of peace namely:

1. *Inner Peace* - the peace an individual has in himself and herself, i.e., peace with body, mind, soul, and spirit.
2. *Peace with People* - In the family, in the workplace, and in the community, and peace with other religions, ethnicities and nations.
3. *Peace with the Environment* - Reverence for nature and animals and to have a sustainable society.
4. *Peace with God* - or with whatever other name the individual believes in—such as The Benign, Intelligent, Creative Power—that is behind it all, which goes by such as God, Allah, Brahman, etc.

In service to earth and humanity,
Claes Nobel

MESSAGE FROM WOLFGANG DIETRICH

Swami Veda Bharati is without any doubt one of the wisest personalities of the 21st century. His enormous knowledge in religious and philosophical matters has inspired generations and enriched many, including the students of the UNESCO Chair for Peace Studies at the University of Innsbruck in Austria.

His new book is a particular important contribution to world peace because it unites the Swami's spiritual trans-culturality with an optimist opinion on the human potential to a trans-rational approach in the very sense of the word. Hence it empowers everybody who wants to learn about conflict transformation and, in doing so, it gives an enlightening combination of symbols and notions of peace in many cultures. I thank the author for this jewel.

Prof. Dr. Wolfgang Dietrich,
UNESCO Chair of Peace Studies
University of Innsbruck, Austria

INTRODUCTION

This word-gift is a collection of presentations and essays composed from time to time for different conferences and discussions. It is an attempt to define holism and its application in the interpretation and practice of religion, statecraft, education, and relationships.

Whatever is presented here is received from the founts of ancient wisdom, with no claim to original discoveries in truth, just a reminder to ourselves that alternatives to dissentions and conflicts stand waiting to be beckoned in order to make this planet a harmonious unity and entity.

This presenter invites all readers to disagree and challenge the theses presented here. In response to such challenge, this author would like to bring to mind a paragraph from the Preface titled "Where the Mind Is without Fear," as follows:

> Dissenters and disputants will learn the art of merger of diverse faces of truth, each one learning to stand where the opponent stood, and shall espouse the other's cause against one's own. In other words, by taking the opponent's side, I hope to complete for myself the truths left incomplete in these writings.

May all opposites in the universe be seen as complementary and thus help to complete us who are yet incomplete beings in spiritual evolution. I would like to add a note on the choice of the title and subtitle of this book.

One may ask why choose *"What Is Right With The World?"* My answer is that what is wrong with the world is a very popular complaint of many persons. We need to look on the positive side of life and recognize those things that are going "right." As far as the title is concerned, I have decided to use the word "urge" instead of "yearning," or any other such words, because the natural urge to peace is an almost instinctive nature of the human being. Yearning is not the same as an instinctive urge.

Give way to your natural human urges—the urge to give, the urge to share, the urge to make sacrifice for others, the urge to knowledge, the natural urge to peace.

I have often said that as we grow spiritually, the sense in which we use words changes. People think that we are speaking with a meaning that they attribute to the word, but we are saying something entirely different. For example, the word "urge" is often used in the sense of base urges, but sublime urges are forgotten. Here we use the word as referring to the sublime.

It is my hope that after reading this book, we will have a greater understanding not only of what is right with the world, but how the beauty of that which is right can be applied to beautify what has become ugly in so many eyes.

May the reader enjoy what is beautiful with the world.
Swami Veda Bharati

Where the Mind Is without Fear

Where the mind is without Fear,
Let my country[1] awake.
    Rabindranath Tagore

Perennial in the Millennium (Veda Bharati, 1999) was composed in
Johannesburg, South Africa, as a message to accompany the celebrations
that would welcome the Third Millennium of the Christian era. Many read
it as a poetic composition, but it was actually meant to be a manifesto for a
complete and total holism. The word "holistic" is used here to indicate:
(a) that all of humanity, not divided into factions of religions, nations, and
ethnicities, has a common spiritual goal; (b) that all aspects of the human
individual and collective life forms are an integrated whole, (c) that this
holistic spirituality needs to, and can, become the common holy ground
for all; and (d) that all human pursuits, even pursuits such as medicine
and sports, can be felt in the hearts of the participants as parts or aspects
of the single sacrament that is life.

May each member of the *homo contemplatiens[2]* species be a priest of
this sacrament:

"Prophet, Soothsayer, Sage,
What will the next thousand years be like?
I did plant thorn bushes;
Won't you bless me with lilies as I wander in this time path?

1

I made of my offspring marauders.
Won't you pray for them to be wise,
So they flourish, prosper, and sweeten the bitter seas?
Will they, or will they not?
What will the next thousand years of my generations be like?
Prophet, won't you prophesy?

The prophet from the divine thunder roars;
The sage within our soul whispers.

The next thousand years will be whatever you have chosen today to make of them.

Uproot the thorn bushes now; plant lilies instead and the time paths of your generations will be paved with soft, fragrant petals, each petal an achievement from your labor at interior purifications.

Sweeten your minds and the waters of the earth will remain sweet, and be sweeter still by the year.

The plants and trees will flourish, will provide shade, yield fruits, hold the soil together to fasten the clay against erosions and rampant floods; the plentiful herbs will remain potent to grant remedies for illnesses.

The earth's breast will be suckled and not be cruelly dug into, nor shall Gaia[3] be sold as a slave girl for the price of a puff of chimney smoke.

The streams and waters will flow fresh and clear, granting life to all whose roots or lips sip of them gently. The rains will quench and soothe and not burn the skin or scorch the vestment.

The earth's blue silk scarf will wave unstained and unfurl the vigor that only Mother's love can confer.

Nutrition will be obtained from foods freshly gathered without hurt and violence, not dripping blood, nor sucking the life from those who till the earth, and this food will nourish as accorded by the season, first your mind and thereby the physical self.

Our brother kingdoms of the four-footed, the winged, those who crawl on their belly, and those that dive with fins, shall not be held captive, nor shall any from our kingdom spill their blood, neither for gluttony nor for a warped urge of recreation. The human species, having forgotten the smell of fear, all species shall roam in amity with humanity with cordial right of way mutually accorded.

Relationships shall be nurtured so as to pay all one's debts, to learn from those in a different age group, gender, and family station, and not for one wielding power and the others tremblingly yielding to reasonless display. The law of love will enforce itself, needing no exterior enforcers. Virtue shall be its own power of defense, needing no defender.

The matters of polity will provide occasion to test one's inclination for consensus and not to confront and contest. Any contests will be to test one's own depth in virtue.

Humanity shall embark on expeditions of unceasing conquests over its interior maligning forces, driving deep the one-pointed lances of silence.

All the boundaries dividing the earth shall have crumbled the way all walls have crumbled before. All regimes will have fallen; only the cultures shall govern themselves in mutual honor and sharing of all that is inspired.

Everything in the polity, economy, commerce, community, and social order shall be established so as to be conducive to the bond of affection within a family unit, and all that may cause rupture therein will be scrupulously avoided in law and in love.

The children will be honored for their purity, not that their wings be clipped in mid-sky-soaring, nor shall entertainments sully their white mantles of innocent light. The primary teaching will be to help cultivate a personal philosophy of life, and the secondary to enjoy the pleasure of living by that philosophy, and the highest education will be the realization of the spiritual self.

Education will be designed to free the souls from the bondage of the identities of matter. It shall not be a privilege of the few, empowering of the yet fewer, enslaving of many to the drudgeries of the meaningless pursuit simply to provide bread to a starving table. Women, philosophers, and sages will educate with assistance from the instructors who are guided by love to an intuitive entry into the hearts of their minds' beloved children.

Because the ancient mind arts will be revived en masse, the knowledge of all sciences shall be gained in very short time periods, not weighing the minds down with burdensome loads but gaining access to the hidden chambers by the shortest route.

Those who delve into the mysteries of nature's realities and discover truths unknown before shall link them also to an unveiling of the mysteries of the spirit's realities, so that the soul shall give life to the bodies of sciences.

No group shall be denied entry into the ceremonial, ritual, celebration, sacrament of another, nor shall any criticize or be forced to adopt whatever is alien to one and is fulfillment for another. Nevertheless, all shall respect in reverence any alien thought, word, act, or person.

All religions will share space in the same temple-synagogue-cathedral-mosque, all congregating side by side, and each worshipping by his book, his revelation. Each shall thus honor in reverence the priest and the celebrant, the monk and the devotee of the other. All will sing glory to saints of all centuries, of all the chosen peoples, making votive offerings of silence or of song, knowing God by No-name, and by all Her names.

The bards and poets, and not analysts, will preserve the epic and the song that they will sing and recite by heart by bonfires burning all night in all villages, communities, and suburbs, nor shall any tongue be considered lesser than any other.

The entire humanity will tirelessly dedicate itself to collecting, preserving, and passing on as invaluable inheritance all wise and sacred texts. Each individual will value these repositories of knowledge as wealth to be gathered, as gems to be treasured.

Recreation and entertainment shall be an enriching of the soul's beauty and not a restive commotion produced from and feeding the mind's cravings for the unnameable, momentary, fleeting satisfactions by sensation. Trading in human bodies shall have ceased, for all will worship the soul housed in this form. So shall commerce in sport be abolished, in order for sport to be an enrichment of human value.

Knowing the body's cure to be in the body and the whole person's health in the mind, the malignancies of negative emotions shall first be prevented and then eliminated if still risen. By the juice of the whole herb and the root shall the body's wellness saps be nurtured, by harmonious nutrition enriched, and they shall not be weakened by unguarded indulgence.

The light in the mineral, the ambrosia in the thorn, weed, and thistle, and the nectar in the venom shall be extracted by the sanguine to oil life's flame, to add liquid luster to every fluid drop that courses in the vein— in season, by the lunar phase, with prayer seeking permission to take the least not plundering to extinction. Currents of energies, guided by the waves generated in the deep repositories of the mind and brain, shall be re-channeled to impart to every cell and organ the glow of health and the blessing of longevity.

Speech will be soft, not carrying ego-nurtured assertiveness, nor threatening, nor louder, nor more verbose than absolutely necessary for benevolent effectiveness.

The crafts will fulfill the soul's longing for beauty, the goods produced to cater to need and never for greedy hoarding. Nor shall possessions be the measure of a person's worth but of his capacious heart given to sharing in charity and love. Nor shall position be an exhibit of power but a way to satisfy the innate urge to serve in humbleness of love.

Occupations and the economies will be pursuits to add to the earth's green mantle, to help all to savor the opportunities for beauteous creativity devoted to granting comfort to the relatively deprived. Nor shall any fetus suffer from absence of micro-nutrition, nor shall a single seasoned aged elder curl up to sleep hungry, alone, uncared for. There shall be no wasting of the surplus, thereby no dearth of the essential.

The cities of today shall be remembered as cancers that have been cured, all cells restored, life saps replenished. People shall make their dwellings least visible, partially underground, and above these shall flourish green gardens where the beings of all kingdoms of the earth roam freely, lounge in the shades of trees, drink amply of the streams, and be restored to invigorating freshness.

This past millennium shall be remembered as the dark ages bereft of enlightenment, this cluster of centuries as the most destructive ever, the memory of which causes not a savor but a shudder. The nations that war inside each human skull shall have signed a treaty of perpetual peace within, and thus shall the specter of war, famine, untreated disease, and the shelterlessness cease for the vast masses whose hurt will now be assuaged with prevalence of love as the primary qualification for the masters, nay, the wisdom-endowed guides, of polity.

Science and soul having been reunited to be conducive to human affections, all work will be done through vastly refined electronics and communicated by means of harmless rays. Nor shall any human endeavor cause to pour even a particle of killing poison into the air held sacred.

Men and women shall worship each other's beauteous souls that have rendered their forms so magnetically charged. It is in worship that they will learn to unite. From such a union that is a sacrament offered to Divinity, the future generations shall be brought forth in consideration of the earth's resources.

Dissenters and disputants will learn the art of merger of diverse faces of truth, each one learning to stand where the opponent stood, and shall espouse the other's cause against one's own.

All that was considered opposite heretofore shall be revealed as complementary, to be savored in its richness, so that the mind shall not be coerced into having to choose between night and day but shall value equally the day's lights and the night's silences, even carrying light into the night and bringing forward silence into the day, for life's completeness.

Whether the human embarks on adventures into outer space or stays firmly rooted on earth, his journey into vast internal spaces shall be his primary adventure. Here in the depths of this interior sky one shall view wonders of micro-worlds and macro-universes of uncountable varieties.

Beings shall live, not by the contemporary temporal, nor by the restricted spatial, but by the ever-expansive perennial.

Each individual will value and preserve all that is conducive to harmony, gentle thought, beauteous speech, modest claim, and realization of the spiritual self within.

The human kingdom shall lay no claim to the possession of the planet.

In trust alone shall we hold it, for civilization will be governed by the love and wisdom of the woman, by the understanding of the philosopher, by the vision of the sage and the saint.

And it shall be so, because minds will have been guided into a contemplative, self-observant, aware habit, and their meditations will have replaced all the negative images that sully the stream of clear reason, pure intuition, and grace of revelation.

It shall be so henceforth. So shall it be in the year 3001, if you so choose to make it.

Grace and blessing of Divinity's Infinity, and of all Her Mind's children, the saints of all ages and peoples, will guide, nourish, and nurture the millennium if you will it so in surrender to the Perennial.

The lily petals of your meditations will make your time paths, and of all the generations to come, beauteous and fragrant.

Such shall be the next millennium, if you simply will it so.

CHAPTER I
Unifying Streams in Religions

In studying the history of humanity, the development of political and economic power is often emphasized predominantly. The role of religion, on the other hand, is most often seen as adjunct or secondary to these forces. This perspective results in looking at religion as mostly allied with the divisive political and economic concentrations of power. Religion, however, also exists apart from such forces, and there it bears quite a different fruit. It is, indeed, important to examine the mistakes made by religions in the past, but it is also imperative that religion serves as a guide to establishing peace, nonviolence, unity, and harmony. We learn from those aspects of the religious past that have often successfully contributed to the achievement of these more desired goals.

Similar Streams of Worship In Religions
What follows is a view of religion as an instrument of harmony, a view that has been known, but one that has not been examined as a universal and cohesive stream that has run through all ages and areas of world history. By looking at the successes of religion in establishing peace in the past, we can prepare a plan for the future.

Various kinds of dialogues and conferences in different parts of the world are presently searching for ways in which the world's religions may find a common ground to help guide humanity in a positive direction, even though such a shared ground has been recognized, and even established, for thousands of years by ordinary people as well as by sages, saints, philosophers, and theologians. It can, in fact, be said that there exists a vast treasury of experience in the area of unifying the religions, with regard to both a theoretical framework established by philosophers, saints, and sages on a didactic basis, as well as shared spiritual experience. In addition, in daily life, experiments in peaceful coexistence have been successfully conducted by the common people in a practical and pragmatic realm, often independent of theories and theologies.

The shared elements addressed by the following 20 questions, both selectively and by way of illustration for argument's sake, are well known, but they have not previously been strung together in a unified theory demonstrating the common streams that link various religions. In so doing, however, the presence of a single unifying stream flowing through all periods of time and locations is revealed.

1. In which inter-religious council of the world was it agreed upon that Hindus, Buddhists, and Christians of all denominations would join their hands before their hearts in worship?
2. Who decreed that people of almost all faiths should kneel or bow in one form or another to the presence of Divinity?
3. Is it a meaningless coincidence that so many mudras (gestures and positions) of body, face, and hands are very similar in the icons of Jesus, the Buddha, and the Hindu forms of the Deity? The same is true of the Virgin Mary, Kuang Yin[1], and Divine Mother figures such as Saraswati and Lakshmi[2].
4. When was it agreed upon by various religions that prayers should be counted on rosary, mala, or tasbeeh[3] by the Christian, Hindu, Buddhist, Taoist, or Muslim?
5. Who determined that sacred and holy water, whether from the Jordan, Ganga, or Zamzam,[4] should be an important component of religious observances for the Christian, Hindu, Buddhist, Taoist, and Muslim?
6. Which master architect planned all edifices for worship to point upward and into the sky?
7. When was the agreement signed that incense be burned in sacred places of the Hindu, Buddhist, American Indian, Muslim, and Catholic?

8. How is it that ringing a bell has been part of a ritual among so many different forms of worship in different religions?
9. Who determined that meatless days be observed by the adherents of many religions?
10. Is it strange that what the Asian religions (Hinduism and Buddhism) refer to as dashansha (a tenth of one's income to be donated) is considered an equally important duty as tithing in Western religions?
11. Who decided that periods of forty days are optimum for those seeking purification, whether Hindu, Buddhist, Muslim (as in the practice of chilla[5]), Kadazan[6], or the Christian observing Lent?
12. Who enjoined the practice of silence and fasting for all devotees of God?
13. Who determined that people of most faiths should say grace before meals?
14. How was it agreed upon by the people of all traditions that women, children, and unarmed soldiers or civilians should not be attacked in a war?
15. Who taught that an immersion in a holy river would constitute a spiritual rebirth?
16. How is it that so many rituals of a monk taking his vows, such as tonsure, are so similar among the Hindu Swamis and Buddhist and Christian monks, when the histories of their monastic orders are of divergent antiquities?
17. Who developed the idea that the followers of each religion should have a sacred book, in written or oral form?
18. Who instituted the tradition of song as an offering to Divinity in all religions?
19. How is it that as part of "a floating mass of wisdom," the people of all religions tell parables and stories that parallel each other, one claiming it to be Hindu, another calling it Sufi, or Buddhist, or Christian?
20. How is it that we find almost identical passages in the Popul Vuh (Recinos, Goetz, & Morley, 1965), the Bible (Holy Bible, 1982), the Qur'an (Ali, 1995; Maududi, 1996),[7] Mahabharata

(Narasimhan, 1965),[8] Dhammapada (Carter & Palihawadana, 1998),[9] Avesta (Geldner, 1986),[10] and the Upanishads (Ekadasopanisadah, 1966; Hume, 1971)?[11]

As an international team of researchers on global warming at Lake Suwa in Japan has reported (*International Herald Tribune*, 2000), the deities from shrines on either side of the shore of the frozen lake "were believed to have used surface ice to visit back and forth," and at Lake Constance, on the border of Germany and Switzerland, "congregations at two churches, one in either country, had the tradition of carrying a Madonna figure back and forth across the lake after it froze." What power might be involved here that unites the adherents of Shinto (the traditional religion of Japan that holds all natural phenomena as imbued and made alive with their corresponding deities or Kamis) with the Christian tradition?

Likewise, what common connection joined the proto-pashupati[12] of Mohenjo Daro[13] with the scenes depicted on the Gundestrup cauldron from distant Denmark? How did the Druids (ancient priest-judges and scholar-teachers of the Celtic tradition), the Brahmins, and the followers of Pythagoras (see Ovid's, *Metamorphoses*, (1986) Chapter 15) all develop a faith with so many similarities while living in lands so distant from one another? Where shall we look for the common source of the Vestal Virgins,[14] the Virgin Mother of Jesus, the Virgin Saraswati,[15] the Virgin Wise Woman of the Oneida,[16] and the Kumari institution[17] of contemporary Nepal?

Can we not simply acknowledge that these common streams among religions have always flowed in freedom, irrespective of the social, political, and other repressive forces active at the time? All we need do is to acknowledge and identify the power of these streams in order to chart the course for the flow of our own river in history into the future.

There are Divine or transcendent forces, besides the human ones, that are the fountainhead from which the human urge to worship proceeds, and that teach all of the "chosen peoples" in all centuries and nations the ways to worship as well. It is the presence of these forces that comprises the unifying stream among all of our religions. This is not simply evidence of Carl Jung's (1981) notion of the collective unconscious, but, rather, it is from deep personal spiritual experience that all branches of humanity have been guided in tandem and parallel streams throughout history. It is because of this common source in the Divine Forces that so many symbols, verbal and art forms, and rituals are shared among religions. I pay homage to these Forces of No-names and All Names.

Streams of Common Inspiration

Religion is experienced internally, and is expressed and shared externally, to influence social functions at many different levels simultaneously. This is so because religion derives its impulse from many different areas and states of the human mind that do not often operate cohesively. Yet in the background there remains a trans-mental divine and spiritual source from which it originates as revelation and inspiration. But the original inspiration often becomes sullied. Divergences could enrich. Instead, they often divide because of the closed states of mind of later followers. The common stream of inspiration, however, is never lost and continues to show itself throughout human experience, guiding human beings to much that is noble, beautiful, nonviolent, harmonious, and infinitely loving.

The purpose here is not to psychoanalyze religion by looking at the cause of its failure, but to learn, for the future, from its past successes. We need not make the attempt to negate the negations in order to arrive at the positive, nor deny the effects of those negations. This proposal is not to examine the well-known weaknesses once more, but rather to recognize and reinforce inherent strengths.

It may appear that the failures of our favored path are being ignored in order to selectively bring forward some isolated instances of success to justify religion. That is not what is intended. If a certain type of event is seen repeating itself in many lands and over many centuries, producing an identical mental experience and consequential social effect, then it needs to be studied to identify the common denominator. Let us look, therefore, at commonly repeated patterns of truth, goodness, and beauty manifested in history through religion, so that they may be understood and better applied.

The alliances of the adherents of religions with divisive political and economic powers are ignored here, because this has been amply elaborated upon by many analysts. We, instead, propose to look at the widely scattered events in which mystics and philosophers, the common people, and even some powerful political personages have maintained the shared experience of religion as a force for harmony. The examples cited here are sketchy and the list is not exhaustive. These are just examples to be knitted into a holistic pattern, and then included in any projections of the future. The patterns found in society as a whole will be viewed first, so as to apply the results of these studies to the more pragmatic world of today.

Streams of Merging

It is well known that in plural societies, where a number of separate ethnic communities coexist, the common people, being exposed to the experience of each other's belief systems and practices, often manage to merge them. People begin by sharing experiences and practices out of neighborly courtesy. This they manage to do without diluting their own basic belief systems. They accommodate the divergent only to the extent that no major infringement of their own faith occurs. They often compromise with minor infringements. Quite frequently fresh myths appear to justify such mutual accommodation at the level of the "little traditions."

It is common in the villages of India, for example, for Hindus to savor sevai (vermicelli dessert) on the occasion of the Muslim Eid festival, and for Muslims to share sweets in celebration of Divali (the Hindu Festival of Lights). In Guyana, some Afro-Guyanese join in the celebration of Phagwa (the Hindu Festival of Colors), and in Fiji, kava (an indigenous Fijian drink) is served at most Indian celebrations. The indigenous Fijian deity Nakovandra has become identified as a divine Naga[18] (Hindu) figure, and this Naga image is commonly placed near the entrance of Shiva[19] temples, as nagas are known to be Shiva's ornaments. In some Hindu versions of the myth of Krishna[20] dancing on the head of Kaliya Naga,[21] it is stated that Krishna banished the naga to a ramanaeeka dveepa, a charming island. What island could be more charming than Fiji? Maybe it was to Fiji that Krishna banished Kaliya (the name of the naga). Myths take many such local forms.

The Indian folk singers of Surinam, Guyana, Trinidad, Mauritius, and Fiji often begin their song session with verses like:

Hinduon ko ram-ram.
Christians ko good day.
Musalmanon ko salaam.

Ram Ram to the Hindus.
Good Day to the Christians.
Salaam to the Muslims.

The songs sung in rituals may be adapted from one religion to fill a need in another. The Hindu folk singer sings:

Oh, under what tree might Rama and Lakshmana,[22] both brothers in exile, be sheltering and getting all drenched? The Shia Muslim folk singer, whose ancestors might have converted from Hinduism to Islam, sings at Muharram:
Oh, under what tree might Hasan and Husain,[23] both brothers in exile, be sheltering and getting all drenched?

Such songs may still be heard on the festive and sacramental occasions of Islam in Lahore and other Pakistani cities, and the spring festival Basant is celebrated with equal gusto by the Muslims of Lahore and the Hindus and Sikhs of Amritsar, on opposite sides of the border. What diehard Hindu has not at one time or another enjoyed the Muslim devotional songs of qavvali?[24]

The famous Muslim monument called chaar meenaar in Hyderabad, India, shares a corner wall with a Hindu temple. The significance of this is provided by an interview with Ziauddin Tucy, the great-grandson of the last Moghul, Bahadur Shah Zafar, published in the *Times of India* (2000):
I asked Ziauddin Tucy about Hyderabad. Has it changed? "Yes, it has lost its cultural identity." What was this cultural identity all about? "It was about the love and cordiality between Hindus and Muslims. I, as a child, would sit for days in the Ganesh puja pandals (temporary tents built for worship) and participate in the festivities. Now this doesn't happen." What has brought about this change? "Siasat, politics."
We sit in silence for a while. "You see, Jodha Bai was a Hindu. She was

15

Salim's mother. Bahadur Shah Zafar's mother was Lal Bai, again a Hindu." Do you believe that the warmth between the Hindus and Muslims has come to an end? "No, it is there, but parde ke pichhe hai. It is behind a curtain."

On the same day, the same newspaper devotes three columns to a report, of which the following is an excerpt:

"Muslim Chief in Orissa State of India Presides Over Vijayadashmi Yajna"

Manikgada (Orissa). Durga Puja[25] is a festival celebrated [only] by Hindus. [This is] wrong, for in this village, about 90 kilometers. from Bhubaneshwar, Muslims celebrate it with as much reverence and solemnity as their Hindu brethren.

There is also more to this festival in this village. For generations, the prasad is brought from the house of the village chieftain, who is a Muslim, and is first offered to [the] goddess Durga. The chieftain also presides over a mass yajna[26] on Vijayadashmi, while Hindus and Muslims distribute the prasad among themselves.

On the last day of the puja[27] (Vijayadashami),[28] thousands of Muslims from nearby villages throng Manikgada to witness the last procession of [the] Goddess Durga that starts from the tribal temple located right in front of a mosque. The procession first halts before the chieftain's house, where the goddess is offered prasad.

The village chieftain, Sheikh Habibur Rehman, says: "… I fast on Dashami and eat the Prasad."[29]

A villager, Juber Mahammad, adds: "Since most of our forefathers were paikas (soldiers with the king) like the Hindus, we worship the swords and other arms on the occasion of Dashami. It has become our major festival."

In the most recent Gujarat earthquake (January, 2001), Haji Bhura, a practicing Muslim, continues to guard "The Mahavir Swami Temple, the second most important pilgrim centre of Jains[30] in Gujarat." He convinced his quake-stricken wife and two sons that his presence in the temple was more necessary than being with them. "My job is to protect this temple," he said. "I cannot run away. My Allah is watching me (*Times of India,* 2001).

There are numerous such instances not only in India, but throughout the world.

One can only wish that the attitudes of all peoples in the world could be shaped by the spirit of such news items.

Another news item headline states:

"A Muslim Helps to Restore Temple in Uttar Pradesh"

Ali, a devout Muslim observing roza and offering namaz five times a day, is setting an example of Hindu-Muslim unity in a village in Uttar Pradesh. He has not let his faith come in the way of his mission to renovate a 400-year old Devi Mandir at Ghurharipur on the banks of the Ghaghra. The mission started by him three years ago has earned him the support of others of his faith such as the local youths (Times of India, 2009a).

Another news item reported how Hindus were delaying the ringing of temple bells to accommodate their Muslim brothers' prayers or namaz during the Ramadan period, so as not to disturb them. This was a mixed community sharing the same building (*Times of India,* 2009b).

Why is it that in reporting on Hindu-Muslim relations most observers fail to mention the Muslim singers who, even in Delhi, sing of Shiva, and the Muslim singers in Surinam, Guyana, and Trinidad who sing the Bhojpuri and Hindi bhajans[31] of Rama and Krishna, including the compositions of Tulasidas,[32] to crowds of thousands? And why forget the numerous learned Muslim devotees, like Malik Muhammad Jayasi and Abdur Rahim Khanekhana, who composed mystical epics on Sufi-Yogi-Hindu themes and songs of devotion to Krishna? Let us also not forget the Muslim classical dhrupad[33] singers who have, to this day, kept a Vedic tradition alive. One of the most popular bhajan singers in India who has sung to Krishna at the famous Hindu Guruvayur shrine (in Tamilnadu) is a Christian with the name of Yesudas, servant of Jesus. Nor should we ignore the indigenous Fijians who sing Hindi songs.

On Rajpur Road in Dehradun, where I lived for many years, I wit-

17

nessed a Hindu roadside shrine of the Hindu Pahalwan Baba being worshipped by both Hindus and Muslims. Further up in Rajpur village there is a mazaar (grave of a Muslim saint) where both Hindus and Muslims go to offer prayers and thanks for wishes fulfilled. There are innumerable examples of such mixed attendances at these shrines. No one bothers whether he or she is Hindu or Muslim. They go to worship for the sanctity the shrine provides.

In Shivpuri colony in Dehradun for the past 25 years, a secular charity organization, KHEL (Kindness, Health, Education, and Laughter), has managed to maintain peace and harmony among the diverse populations of Hindus, Muslims, Sikhs, and Christians simply by inviting friendly dialogues and promises for calm whenever violence between these groups happens elsewhere.

Common Streams in Different Countries

Indonesia offers one of the most impressive illustrations of how various religions may join together to create a harmonious lifestyle and a unified cultural psyche. In the Indonesian version of the secular, the priests of all religions are paid by the state. It has been made compulsory that if even a single child of a particular religion studies at a school, he or she must be given lessons in his or her own religion, and this is done through state support. Nepi Day, the day of silence observed by the Balinese Hindus, is a national day of silence for the followers of all religions throughout Indonesia. Many books are available on the subject of how the Muslim religion and the traditions represented by the Ramayana (Buck, 1976) and the Mahabharata have co-existed in that vast country for so many centuries. Even though today Indonesia is a mainly Muslim nation, because of its Hindu heritage, a sculpture of a famous scene from the Bhagavad Gita (Radhakrishnan, 1948; Shankaracarya, 1977) depicting Arjuna and Krishna in a chariot stands in the middle of the city of Jakarta.

Often an accommodation is made to insert the traditions and forms of an older religion into the new religion of a conqueror, or of one who evangelizes a local population. An example is the continuity of the tradition of the Christmas tree in Christianity, even though Odin and Thor[34] have been abandoned and Jesus has replaced them. The two divergent streams are unified, and one cannot say where one ends and the other begins. The Christians in Rome adopted forms of the Roman religion into their rituals; the Christian Greeks maintained many of the original Greek forms. The Christians settling in Kerala in South India adopted the rituals of worship from their surroundings. Many major elements of their sacraments and ceremonies, where they would not conflict with the tenets of their own faith, are identical to the ones practiced in the surrounding Hindu society. This process of amalgamation continued from the first to the 16th century A.D. and was resumed again after India's Independence.

Even the forms of a chosen deity remain versatile. The Buddha figures of Mathura, Gandhara, Korea, China, and Japan, or of the traditions of the Khmer, Lao, or Thai, each exhibit the features of the people of the respective land. The concept of a black Christ in Africa is well known, and Mother Mary in Kerala wears a sari. The same Divine Mother of the universe in Her 21 aspects is worshipped as Tara in India (and in the maritime regions of Indian civilization), Dolma in Tibet, Kwang Yin in China, and Kwannon in Japan. The same Sanskrit mantra is transmitted by the Hindu worshippers of Tara and by the Buddhists of the Sino-Japanese civilization. This is also true of various other mantras. The mantra of the "Hindu" Saraswati (a female form of the Deity) is also transmitted as the mantra of Manjushri (the Buddha of Wisdom).

Even the word Om is held sacred by four religions—Hindu, Buddhist, Jain, and Sikh—with different meanings in accordance with the doctrine of each faith. In the philosophy of the Upanishads, Om expresses the One Unmanifest and the three manifest states of consciousness (dreaming, sleeping, and wakefulness), whereas in Buddhism it represents the merging of the body, speech, and mind of the devotee with those of the Buddha. The Jains see in it the Five Holy Ones of their faith represented by the initial letters a, u, and m. The Five Holy Ones are honored in the basic, five-fold sacred mantra of the Jains: arihantas/enlightend beings; siddhas/adepts; ayariya/noble people; uvajjhaya/living teachers; sadhus/ ascetics and monks.

Some liturgical and ritual forms, relevant to the doctrines and practices of one religion are found in another, where they have no relevance. For example, take the formula "ashes to ashes, dust to dust." In the Christian tradition, "dust to dust" is relevant as bodies are buried in the dust, but what is the relevance of "ashes to ashes?" This part of the formula could be applicable only in cultures and religions where cremation is the normal practice.

As part of the consecration of oneself, the vibhuti (sacred ashes) is applied to the forehead and other parts of the body with the Vedic recitation:

Fire – that is ashes
Air – that is ashes
Water – that is ashes
Ground – that is ashes
Space – that is ashes

All of this [universe-phenomena] is indeed ashes; even the mind and these senses [are ashes].

This is reinforced in the Veda again when it says:

Bhasmantam shariram
The body ends in ashes.
Yajur Veda (40.17) (e.g., Keith, 2008; Uvvata & Sharma, 1912)

However, the institution of Ash Wednesday and the idiom "sackcloth and ashes," as the way of the ascetic and the penitent, echoes the more elaborate application of ashes in the traditions of India where, as in the ceremony of Ash Wednesday, the marks of a particular faith are applied with the thumb and are placed on the forehead with the recitation of liturgical formulae. One may also compare the Lenten veil before the sanctuary with a similar curtain drawn before a Hindu altar between sessions of worship. These examples are incomplete, but sufficient here.

Buddhists of Central Asia converting to Islam brought many Buddhist ideas, including that of the Null (transcendental Nihil, equivalent of the Buddhist concept of shunya, the transcendental Void), into the Sufi tradition. The Sufis met the Shaivites of Kashmir and were honored with the title of rishi, a realized sage, through whom divine revelation flows. One such rishi was Nooruddin, whose shrine, the charar shareef, is venerated by people of both faiths, the Muslim converts and the Shaivites. The descendants of the Maya, Inca, and Aztec peoples superimposed Catholic saints upon their old deities to conceal their continued worship of them, and merged elements of the ancient ritual into that of the new. The same experiment is now taking place in Africa, where the indigenous belief systems of the many nationalities of Africa first accommodated the practices of Islam and now are doing the same with Christianity. The Yoruba[35] brought their Orixa deities to the New World where, as slaves, they were forced to convert to Christianity. But they merged the two traditions, producing such enrichments as the Santeria of Cuba and Condamble of the Bahia region of Brazil.

Quite often the sacred exists and flourishes with reference to different religions simultaneously. The Dome of the Rock is a point of international controversy because it is being made so by those in power in both the states and religions involved. Left to the people, the problem could be solved gently over a period of time. This is not mere speculation about a possibility. In Mauritius, the temple of Mama Tukkai (Durga), reputed to grant miraculous healing and solutions to personal problems, is reverently visited by the Afro-Mauritians. There are thousands of shrines dotting the whole of India where Hindus and Muslims worship together; while a Hindu fire ritual is going on in one corner, a Muslim recitation in Arabic resonates in an adjacent place nearby. In many such shrines, the resident Muslim Faqir,[36] out of respect for the Hindus, does not permit non-vegetarian food. India and Pakistan may be old rivals, but when there is the festival of a Sufi saint, the physical or geographical state borders vanish during the worship that takes place.

Religions often change, but the sacredness is retained. The shrines of indigenous people taken over by theologically more sophisticated religions continue to be sacred. Among the more tolerant lands, even the icons are not replaced.

In other instances, while the site of the religion of the conquered or the converted may be altered into the church, mosque, or temple of the conqueror or the evangelist, the site itself remains sacred, reserved for worship, and now in a new form. The Sun temple of the Incas in Cusco is an example. A hill near the town of Rajagriha where the Buddha lived in a

21

hut close to the Bamboo Grove practicing his austerities, now holds the graves of Muslim divines. Yet the site remains sacred. The civil war in Sri Lanka continues because those who are responsible for the war ignore the genius and wisdom of the people. In spite of the war, it is common there for Buddhists to visit Hindu shrines, and for Hindus to pay homage to the Buddha.

Almost every Chinese person with a strong spiritual belief worships at Taoist as well as Buddhist shrines, and they all pay homage to Confucius. No one tells them that they must choose only one of the two or three religions. Often Taoist deities are enshrined in Buddhist temples and vice versa. A Japanese individual may go to both a Shinto and Buddhist temple, and worship the Kami[37] deities as well as the Buddha with equal devotion. What is more, the images of Hindu origin, like those of Narayana and Ganesha,[38] are still honored there.

The migration of Hindu thought and practices to other parts of Asia is well known. It is common in Nepal, as well as in Bali, to be asked: Are you a traditional Hindu, Buddha Hindu, or Shiva Hindu? This kind of question is not an accident. One of the greatest contributions of Indonesia and of Bali is in this unity of religions. In the year 1011 at a place which is now known as Pura Samuan Tiga there was perhaps the first inter-religious conference of three religions: Shiva, Buddha and Bali Aga, the traditional pre-Buddhist, pre-Hindu, Balinese religion. The scholars and the leaders sat down and worked out a system by which the three religions should work together and exchange forms with each other and that is the religion of Bali today. The success of the resolves that were then made continues to this day. Why is it that the powerful people who comprise the religious councils of today do not look at such successful experiments in human history, learn from them, and re-institute the attitudes that led to such success in the past?

A contemporary scholar who is searching for clues regarding the possible unity of religions would need to examine the processes by which Hindu traditions have merged with, for example, the local Khmer, Thai, or Lao traditions in such a way, that in each of their respective communities, it would be impossible for anyone to identify which drops have come from which stream. What were the processes by which Hindus and Buddhists accommodated each other in the kingdoms of Java? When Islam arrived, how was it that major elements of the older Hindu-Buddhist culture continued to remain prominent within the framework of Islam? To a large extent they visibly still continue to do so, as evidenced by, for example, the sculpture of Arjuna[41] and Krishna in Jakarta mentioned above.

One of the major experiments in forming a unifying stream in religions has been conducted in India for many thousands of years, where Hindus, Buddhists, and Jains have constantly interacted. It has been said that Buddhism has disappeared from India, but this is not so! Buddhist tenets were absorbed into the Hindu view of life and practices, just as Hindu forms of the deity were included in Mahayana Buddhism in mainland India, its maritime regions, and in Tibet. In India, the Jains and the Zarathustrians both study the Bhagavad Gita with the same diligence as the Hindus, and the Jains offer prayers to the Hindu forms. The shrine in Bodh-gaya, where the Buddha attained enlightenment, is sacred to both Hinduism and Buddhism (although for different reasons), and the people of both religions have worshipped there together for a thousand years. There is, however, a sad situation today in that current political forces, ignoring the people's wishes and inclinations, are creating tension and division between these groups.

The kingdom of Thailand is Buddhist, but its major ceremonies call for the presence of Brahmin priests to officiate. The recent Asiad in Thailand, held under the patronage of the Buddhist king, was inaugurated with the chants of 108 Hindu priests.

A foundational caring and understanding which occurs through a natural process that is not as yet fully understood, reveals itself not only in such instances of unification, but also in other forms. It is appropriate for catastrophes like those of Kosovo to be widely reported, but why is it that only scant attention is paid to those who risk their lives to protect the members of another community—Europeans in the Nazi era who protected the Jews, Hindus, and Muslims who guarded each other's families during the Indo-Pakistan Partition riots, and Serbs who sheltered Albanians? What was their motivation? Without having been schooled in scholarly theories of inter-ethnic dynamics and so forth, have not these people risked their lives for a purpose higher than survival itself? What are the mental processes and spiritual values of a Schindler or a Wallenburg? Events and personalities of a positive kind like these should be studied in depth. It does not suffice to simply condemn the Holocaust. We also need to look at the mind-state of those who did not participate in such abhorrent happenings, and who actively protected the victims with great risk to themselves. It is in understanding that spiritually empowered state, and teaching children to emulate the same, not as an act alone but the experience in and of itself, that we begin the task of rebuilding human attitudes and, thereby, the human condition for the better.

We have cited many examples of ordinary people who share their traditions without being told to do so, without someone working out the means to be employed, the processes to be followed, and the systems to be adhered to, without knowing the theories of social dynamics, and without having learned the lexicon of the most recently accepted manners or ways. It is obvious that there must be some power within religious and spiritual traditions for so many people to have made the kind of accommodations that we have described.

The official leaders of organized forms of religion may denounce such unifying streams in the world's religions, but common people continue to assimilate their differences and work more closely together. Often local leaders, being from among the people, encourage such a merger of traditions, creating forms that are unorthodox in the eyes of the priesthood of each of the separate participating traditions. The separation is bridged gently over a period of time, following some hidden dynamics among the people themselves. It is these dynamics that the rest of the society needs to notice, understand, and then accept as a guide to establishing peaceful relationships among religions.

Such unification does not only occur at the level of ordinary people. The wise ones, philosophers, and mystics have all been led by their contemplations to find the common principles of various streams. They have even accommodated forms of what appears to others as atheism. While many Hindu philosophers disputed with the Buddhists and the Jains over the existence of God, it is noteworthy that at least two of the six schools, of what is commonly termed the Vedic system, do not acknowledge, or at least do not emphasize, the existence of God. Sankhya-yoga[42] seeks a soul's liberation and enlightenment, but is often interpreted as ignoring God. Mimamsa is the most Vedic of the Vedic schools, dedicated to understanding and reinforcing the philosophy of both daily and ritual acts, but it does not accept the need for a deity.

Some Mimamsa philosophers, after giving all of the arguments against the need for a creator God, then end up making statements like "having stated the argument, I shall now have to undertake acts of penitence for this act of denying God." Are we missing something here? All we can say is that these schools deny the existence of a God determined by our definition of the word (see Rama, 1988).

The philosophers who travelled from India to teach in Tibet merged the elements of the Bon Po with their philosophical systems, finding a niche for the former in the framework of the latter.

- Did not the Greeks, much earlier in Gandhara, create a Graeco-Buddhist and Graeco-Brahmin culture?
- Are there any historical suggestions of any resistance to their endeavors to create such a conjoinment?
- How were these accommodations reached?
- How did the Greek and Egyptian religions join together?
- Did not Zeno (Fairbanks, 1898) find the place where Jewish and Greek thought could complement one another?

It is well known that the world's tallest Buddha at Bamian, which was destroyed by the Taliban, was built by the Greeks who shaped the Gandhara culture in what later became the Muslim country of Afghanistan as we know it today. There exists ample evidence of a healthy contact between the Hindu and the Greek philosophical and religious systems. Alexander of Macedonia had no problem with paying his respects to a Hindu Yogi like Calanus.

Great beings like Apollonius of Tyana travelled to India and learned much from the Yogis. The Jewish tradition assimilated certain thoughts from the followers of Zarathushtra. The Graeco-Egyptian tradition produced the Coptic form of Christianity. Graeco-Hindu thought was absorbed into Neo-Platonism. For example, Porphyry, the Neo-Platonist, composed a treatise that spoke against the eating of animal flesh.

At about the same time, Mani of Iran declared himself to be the joint incarnation of Buddha, Zarathushtra, and Jesus, and preached a doctrine of absolute nonviolence. His religion became as widely accepted among many nations in those days as some of our contemporary religions are today.

The dispute between the followers of Vishnu and Shiva was resolved by Hindu sages who presented the Harihara form of the icon that incorporates the features of both these manifestations of the Divinity. All of this speaks to the willingness of both ordinary people and mystics alike to accept the possibility that the many may be true expressions of the One.

We have spoken previously of the Sufi rishis such as Nooruddin. His spiritual influence on the followers of different religious groups is not an isolated example. Century after century, mystics and sages have challenged the claims of superiority made by one religion over another. Kabir comes readily to mind. The ten Gurus of the Sikh faith brought together the wisdom of all religions, and of the preceding saints of various faiths, into one holy book, the first and only truly "secular" and, at the same time, holy, book, the Guru Granth Sahib (Singh, 1989; Veda Bharati, 1998).

The Arabs, and others of the Muslim nations, absorbed and preserved Greek thought and reintroduced it to Europe, helping to bring about the Renaissance. In recent centuries up to modern times, there are examples of individuals like Paterde Nobili who wore the sacred thread of the Brahmin, interpreting its three strands as representative of the Christian Trinity. Among more recent guides are people like Thomas Merton, who observed the common goals of Zen and Christianity. Many contemplative Christian monks, like Father Dechanet, started a search for similarities between Yoga and Christianity. Father Bede Griffiths established a Christian Swami order at his Ashram near Tiruchirapalli, South India.

Among contemporary scholars are individuals like Raimondo Panikkar (1977), who have presented an introduction to a suggested Christological commentary on the Brahma-sutras (Gambhirananda, 1983), and put forward the proposition that texts like the Mahabharata may be seen as a Hindu parallel to the Bible's Old Testament. It is quite possible that some interpretations of certain religions that suggest the presence of intolerance may be modified through deeper study of their holy books. For example, the Biblical quotation "I am the Way, the Light, and the Life" may be understood differently when one realizes that the Aramaic language does not have the definite article "the." Then the statement is not essentially different from the verse in the Bhagavad Gita: "I am their Deliverer from the ocean of the cycles of death."

Political Streams

Having stated that divisive political forces bear much of the responsibility for separation among religions, it must also be said that in the course of history, there have been many kings who searched for the meaning of truth in all religions, or in one way or another tried to reconcile the concept of nonviolence with their statecraft. Akhenaton (Amenhotem IV), in the 13th century B.C., because of his religious conviction, chose not to resort to armed forces. The emperor Khusro of Iran, a follower of Zarathushtra, liberated 40,000 Jews from Babylonian captivity and helped them to rebuild the Temple of Solomon. He also encouraged the Egyptian priests to diligently revive their own forms of worship under his patronage. His son, Dara, followed in his footsteps. Ashoka, in the third century B.C., disbanded his armies and ruled an entire empire by the power of virtue (dharma).[43] He also provided patronage to the followers of different religions, while he himself remained an adherent of Buddhism. One of his foundational edicts reads:

In as much as one criticizes and harms another religion, he thereby harms his own religion.

Harshavardhana the Great[44] honored the saintly of all religions. Changiz Khan called the teachers of all religions to his court in order to find his truth. Finally, one branch of his descendents settled on Buddhism, and, after Changiz's grandson occupied the throne of Khanbalig (Beijing) as a patron of that religion, an era of nonviolence began in Mongolia and China.

Often such policies, based on tolerance and love, are carried out under the guidance of spiritual teachers, just as Kublai Khan was guided by the head of the Sakya school of Tibetan Buddhism. When Kublai Khan offered to make the Sakya school of Buddhism the only one to be recognized, and said that he would command the Tibetans to become followers only of that path, it was his teacher who dissuaded him from doing so in order that all interpretations of the Teaching could flourish.

The Hindu kings of Kerala gave the same land grants for Christian churches that they gave for Hindu temples. This was not perceived as any special generosity or act of tolerance requiring exceptional consideration or deserving particular recognition; it was built into the religious frameworks of the devout kings. It is well recognized that, because of this societal openness, the Jews of India never suffered any of the indignities that were heaped on these people elsewhere. The synagogues built with the land grants given by Hindu kings continue to be maintained by the adherents of these faiths.

The court of Harun-al-Rashid in Baghdad is known to have become the seat where the highest teachers of all religions met and presented their theses. Akbar, the great Moghul, is known and recognized as one who gently brought together the different paths and teachings in spite of great resistance offered by some fundamentalists. He called the synthesis "The Religion of God." Dara Shikoh, great-grandson of Akbar and an initiate of the Sufi path, was martyred partly because of the mystical realizations that had led him to translate the Bhagavad Gita and the Upanishads from Sanskrit into Persian.

In recent centuries, we have seen similar efforts made by other seekers of truth. The Quaker ideal of tolerance and silence is exemplary. This has not been an inactive tolerance, but has given to history great men like William Penn who, with his associates, attempted to reach a settlement or compromise with the indigenous Americans. The Quakers also served as a support group for Gandhi in the South African struggle for equality among the various segments of the population.

The Persian works of Dara Shikoh were translated into various European languages and helped to develop the interest of philosophers such as Schopenhauer (Young, 2005) in the philosophy of the Upanishads, opening European eyes to the beauty of Vedanta. Numerous European philosophers of note studied Indian philosophy as an age of Oriental Romanticism dawned in the Western world.

Long before any swami visited the United States, the transcendentalist writers opened a way for mutual understanding among religions of East and West. To this day, a visitor looking at the map of various geographical features in the Grand Canyon may observe that Dutton, an orientalist who was then the head of the Geographical Survey of the United States, gave to these features names like Manu Cloisters, Buddha Cloisters, Brahma Temple, and so forth.

Also, although many ideas and concepts that had emerged regarding millions of years of the earth's evolution were new to the West, these same ideas and concepts have comprised an integral part of the common thinking in India for quite a long time. Hence, different geological layers in the Grand Canyon were given names like the "Brahma Layer" and the "Vishnu Layer," and the U. S. dollar bill carries on it the image of the pyramid with the eye of truth from the Egyptian tradition.

All this indicates that the coming together of religions is neither a novel idea, nor something difficult to obtain. In our modern times, guides like Gandhi, Martin Luther King, Bishop Desmond Tutu, all apostles of nonviolence, have been spiritually and religiously inspired. Often the ascetic inspired by spirituality conquers the emperor by the strength of his faith.

Teachers of religions have not always sided with orthodoxy. In fact, up to a century ago, all social reforms in various societies of the world were brought about by particular teachers of religion—those brave and saintly ones who were not overcome by the fear of incarceration, torture, or death at the hands of others of their own religion who were closer to the centers of power. The Buddha was a kshatriya[45] prince who abolished the social distinctions among human beings and sided with the democratic forces of the Vajji and Licchavi[46] democratic confederations. Such teachers have usually suffered at the hands of the powerful of their own religions, a fate that the Buddha, because of his high spiritual power, was spared. Saints like Kabirand Nanak challenged the followers of the religions in which they were born.

The social reform movements of 19th century India began with religious teachers who emerged from the higher castes and challenged their own caste peer groups to help uplift the downtrodden ones; Raja Ram Mohan Roy, Swami Dayananda Saraswati, Gandhi, and Subrahmanya Bharatiyar in southern India may be cited as examples. Also, while the attitudes of a large number of male religious guides toward women are only to be abhorred, there are in the history of religion a large number of names of those who have stood by the side of women, and given them their due veneration as incarnations of the Divine Mother. In recent times, let us not forget those non-black priests and bishops who joined forces with the oppressed, and helped lead movements for their freedom.

Why should history only be read as a record of the wrongdoing of religions, and not equally bring to focus the unselfish dedicated ones who have taught the meaning of equality and service by their example? Those who have valiantly suffered persecution because of their faith are as much, or even more, part of the history of religion as the persecutors.

This is being said here to help find inspiration from those spiritually powerful channels in religion that have withstood the corrupting influences of the secularly powerful. There is much to learn here.

Cultural Streams

The role of religious teachers has not been limited to matters of pure spirituality. They have often established guidance for the behavior of society in matters like environmental protection. In many lands, sacred groves, preserved because of a religious belief system, constitute the only remaining forests. These are well protected, not because of a commercial attitude of sustainable development, but because of the sanctity associated with the idea of non-violence towards all living beings. The way of the Kami in Shinto, the worship of the Orixa deities among the Yoruba, the philosophy of the Sangomas,[47] of the American Indian, of the Maori, of the mystics of the original inhabitants of Australia, and the healing doctors of the indigenous people of Africa, all share the view that nothing should be taken from nature without seeking permission and forgiveness, that not an animal could be hunted or a plant or herb reaped without such a prayer. Though Christian now, the traditional herbal doctors of Malagasy and the healing elder ladies of Tahiti still follow this rule.

As long as the traditional concepts of sanctity as taught by the spiritual guides of these societies continue to be applied, their forests and groves continue to flourish. The Bhagavata-purana (Dharasvami, 1983; van Buitenen, 1996) enjoins "Let not even a blade of grass be pulled from the ground." Be it the traditional healing doctor in Malagasay, Tahiti, India, or among the American Indians, not an herb is taken from Mother Earth without asking for forgiveness in special prayers. Shinto priests are sometimes still invited to perform the ceremonies of atonement and prayer for forgiveness before a tree is cut down in Tokyo. The ceremonial staff to be given to a Hindu monk (swami) taking vows (perhaps cognate with a Christian monk's shepherd's staff) is not taken from the plant without first offering prayers and seeking the permission of the plant. Nor does a good ayurvedic physician pluck herbs without following the same rituals.

Credo Mutwa, the Chief of the South African Sangomas, tells us of the severe penalties that were imposed on one who would pollute a stream, or slaughter wantonly against the rules that prohibited killing of specific animals in restricted areas. There exist formal religions in whose teachings "Thou shalt not cut a tree" is enshrined. For instance, the Bishnoi[48] are known to sacrifice their lives to save a tree. Three centuries ago, in one village of Rajasthan, three hundred women and children hugged trees and were cut down along with the trees by those who came to log them for building a palace. Movements like Chipko (Cling)[49] in the Himalayas have sprung from similar faiths and religious belief systems of both the leaders and the common people.

Was there ever a conference among the diverse peoples of all continents to find or establish such unity of views in all the different centuries, at many different levels of cultural sophistication? What gathering of wise elders of the world decided that the earth was to be looked upon as Mother, no matter what words may be used in whichever language for "earth" and "mother?" The words for the sun may be feminine in both Arabic and Japanese, but earth is always mother, even in the folklores of "fatherlands."

By whatever processes, the diverse peoples of the far corners of the world arrived at these points of agreement, and they did this without signing any international treaties and enforcing them with police, armies, or economic and political sanctions. All we need do is recognize the genius of the spiritual guides and the common people without subjecting them to the will of the politically and commercially powerful. Their faith will do the rest, re-establishing and reinforcing the traditional systems with the necessary reshaping of the spiritual and religious forms to create the changed patterns.

The inspiration is ancient and perennial. If these purer and deeply spiritual aspects of religion are examined and revived in our practice of educating people, the modern day problems that we are seeking solutions for will cease to arise.

Common Streams in Theological Texts

As stated above, it would be most beneficial to students of religion seeking guidance for establishing peace to look at such passages in a variety of religious texts. For example, the Christian doctrine of ex nihilo creation might be better understood by delving into the following words:

> This is the account, here it is.
> Now it still ripples, now it still murmurs, ripples, it still sighs, still hums, and it is empty under the sky.
> Here follow the first words, the first eloquence:
> There is not yet one person, one animal, bird, fish, crab, tree, rock, hollow, canyon, meadow, forest. Only the sky alone is there; the face of the earth is not clear.
> Only the sea alone is pooled under all the sky; there is nothing whatever gathered together.
> It is at rest; not a single thing stirs. It is held back, kept at rest under the sky.
> Whatever there is that might be is simply not there: only the pooled water.
> The calm sea, only it alone is pooled.
> Whatever might be is simply not there: only murmurs, ripples in the dark, in the night.
> Only the Maker, Modeler alone, Sovereign Plumed Serpent...
> And of course there is the sky, and there is also the Heart of the Sky. This is the name of the god, as it is spoken...

Popol Vuh

Of the Beginning of old,
Who spoke the tale?
When above and below were not formed,
Who was there to question?
When the dark and bright were obscured,
Who could distinguish?
When matter was inchoate,
How was it perceived?
                    TIAN WEN (QU & FIELD, 1986)

Over the whole of Africa, creation is the most widely acknowledged
work of God...The people hold that "there was nothing before God created the world." (Mbiti, 1969)
    Compare all these with the well-known Creation Hymn of the Rig
Veda (   ):[51]

There was neither being nor non-being then;
there was no movement, nor that upper sky.
                    RIG VEDA (10.29) (KASHYAP, 2003)
    Then we look at the repeated statements in Indian schools of philoso-
phy that the reality is:

Na san nasan na sad asat
Neither being, nor non-being,
nor being-non-being.

The Buddhist shunya, Null, is then explained as being beyond the four-
cornered statement that: "s" is; "s" is not; "s" both is and is not; "s" neither
is nor "is not." It is that Null or Nihil from which creation would have
been understood to have proceeded as the logos becoming cosmos, the
Word (shabda-brahman of the Vedantin and the Sanskrit grammarian
texts) becoming the physical universe. This may be considered one step
beyond ecumenism, depending on the collective sanction of all of the

revelations to help in understanding each other's content, context, intent, and essence.

Many problems in the theology of one religion can be resolved by studying the explanations given in another. For example, the Christian debates about Acts versus Grace can be resolved by studying how the philosophy of Acts as taught by the purva-mimamsa[52] is merged with the philosophy of realization and grace in uttara-mimamsa, as well as texts such as the Bhagavad Gita.

Many times the Christian Church suffered schisms when dealing with questions related to the apportioning of humanity and divinity to Jesus. A full understanding of the avatara theory (that addresses the descent, incarnation, and enfleshment of divinity) of the Hindus, together with the tenet of divyansha-samudhbhava (one born of a part of the divine), which is discussed in wonderful detail throughout the centuries, can be helpful to the Christian theologian. Such an understanding could bring the two religions closer together, not merely in some form of political coexistence, but in a shared doctrine that is now properly understood.

The doctrinal disputes surrounding transubstantiation versus consubstantiation at the Eucharist may be resolved with the help of the Hindu doctrine and ritual practice of prana-pratishtha that claims to invoke the presence of the divine spirit into what otherwise would be deemed an inanimate object.

There was always a doubt as to which of the gospels is true. Hundreds of versions were burned because of the view that if "x" is true, then "non-x" must not be true. But Hindu tradition has always understood that shata-koti, a hundred million versions of the Ramayana sung in all the universes and in different eons, are all correct because God manifests Herself in innumerable ways.

There are well-established tenets in the textual and philosophical traditions of religions to deter disputation. The Bhagavad Gita enjoins:

Do not create confusion of opinions among people; a wise
person who lives in yoga and practices right conduct should
help all to follow their own paths of action (3.26).

The Buddha advised his followers in Brahma-jala-sutta[53] to ignore all questions of theological dispute that do not have a direct bearing upon the search for enlightenment. The ancient sages of the Rig Veda (1.123.7, 186.4; 5.15.4; 6.58.1, 70.3; 7.27.3, 84.1; 10.10.2, 12.6, 64.5) repeatedly sang of Divinity as being vishu-rupa, and, later, as vishva-rupa[54] or multi-morphous. The rishi sang:

Spreading Your Self, expanding like the earth to bear and to fill,
You suckle and watch over all the peoples.
Supporting, sustaining all age groups, and leading them to
ripening of old age,
You are glorious in all spheres, multi-morphous with
Your own Self
RIG VEDA (5.15.4)

This realization of a Supreme Reality as One Self, atman, ever remaining that one indivisible Self and yet taking multifarious forms, could be the basis of a universal doctrine that would unite all religions in a view of "one in many and many in one" (the motto of the Indonesian state), accepting the variety of manifestations revealed to different people at different times.

The One God appears in many forms, He of a thousand heads, a thousand eyes, a thousand feet (Rig Veda, 10.90.1). The vishva-rupa,[55] the universe as the body of One God. The Yogi of the Upanishads sang:

The Deity Who is in the fire, in the waters,
The One Who has entered to dwell in the entire universe,
The One Who is in herbs and plants,
Unto That Divinity we make obeisance.
SHVETASHAVATARA UPANISHAD (2.17) (VEDA BHARATI, 2002A)

We are reminded of these thoughts again and again in ancient wisdom. The insistence on only one planet, one manifestation, and one revelation causes conflict among all the "only ones." To avoid that, we need to hear again what was said in the Song of the Lord:

In whatever way the people approach Me,
so do I respond to them.
In all paths it is My Path that they
are following from all directions.
Whichever form or aspect of Mine do they worship in faith,
Towards that very form or aspect of Mine do
I sustain their faith.
Endowed with that faith and devotion he seeks to worship
the very same form;
Thereby does he reach the goal desired by him as
I grant to him the same.

BHAGAVAD GITA (4.11; 7.21,22)

Here we are not talking of tolerance, co-existence, and such, but a realization on the part of all to recognize the many ways of God, and to honor, venerate, and revere them. The most detailed statement of this philosophy is found in the Jaina doctrine of anekanta-vada, the doctrine of no one end. Reality is not one-ended. Regarding any face of reality and truth, these seven statements can be made:

a. perhaps is;
b. perhaps is not;
c. perhaps is and is not;
d. perhaps indefinable;
e. perhaps is and is indefinable;
f. perhaps is not and is indefinable;
g. perhaps is and is not, and is indefinable.

All of these statements are to be seen as correct as one comprehensive whole. This philosophy is taught as a system of logic and science of nature and spirit by the great philosophers and visionaries of reality, such as Haribhadra Suri and Kundakundacharya.[56]

Mutual Accommodation

Those seeking a way to find mutual accommodation among religions need to study in depth both the Vedic vishwa-rupa philosophy as well as the anekanta doctrine and make it a part of their personal realization process. Schools of theology and comparative religion need to bring these principles into greater focus and make them the central point of teaching unity in diversity.

This is not merely tolerance for another, forced out of fear of violence and destruction, nor is it a mere response to difficult situations created by humanity's ignorance. This is the credo that millions, no, billions, uphold. All that individuals need on this path is the encouragement granted to them by their spiritual guides. This is not meant to "give them freedom," for that is not anyone's to grant, but it is to recognize and respect freedom in law and in love, and to educate future generations into remaining true to these perennial truths. Such an education will not be possible, however, nor will there develop the state of mind that leads to the choice of non-violent inclinations, unless the contemplative heritage of all religions and spiritual traditions is revived.

Methods of contemplation to retrain the mind and ways of meditation seem to be divergent, but there are certain procedures that are common to all systems of meditation. A key advantage of this common, core component of these seemingly different systems is that it can be practiced within the context of all religious traditions without violating any of their tenets. Such practice would strengthen the faith of each individual and, thereby, of each religious community through the purification and clarification of the spiritual mind. May all councils that govern the world begin each of their deliberations with such a meditation, so that a calm, spiritual state of mind be established before undertaking any and all decision-making processes.

In addition, may such meditation practices be introduced and integrated into educational institutions, contributing significantly to the development of beneficial states in the child's mind, states of mind that would preclude and prevent tendencies to violence, aggression, and mutual intolerance. In this way, such tendencies would be dissolved and disspelled at the outset, so that children would grow into adults who are confirmed in and committed to peace, both within themselves as well as all aspects of their lives in the world.

CHAPTER 2
Meditation: The Unifying Stream

This chapter points to humanity's experience of harmony among religions, and the collective need to recognize the strength in wisdom, and the applications of that wisdom, that have brought about such beauty in past periods of human experience.

What follows are the results of a search for examples of some of the common principles and practices in various religions, a search done while remaining cognizant of some of their fundamental differences. This presentation and discussion also takes into account some of the past errors that have been made in mistakenly identifying religions with ethnicities, nations, states, and other mundane interests.

Those who are pursuing the search for unity and harmony among religions need to look at the contemplative paths and meditative traditions, both individually and collectively, in the history of religion. The following explores some of the contemplative methods and systems that are held in common among religions, and suggests that the internal peace of the individual mind generated through meditational practices spills over into society, generating harmony where there has been discord. Societies and communities in strife may, thus, create a cooperative, even convivial, relational atmosphere with the systematic adoption of such calming practices.

Anyone, irrespective of his or her beliefs and physical abilities, can practice meditation to receive its benefits by way of the internal calm that it generates, the efficacy of which has been proven in numerous scientific and medical investigations over the last five decades. True education for peace will begin when training the mind to be calm through the practice of contemplative systems becomes a regular part of the educational system. However, this must be established without prejudice toward anyone's belief in a religious doctrine or the absence thereof. In other words, integrating contemplative practices and meditation into education and training should in no way violate anyone's faith, or denial thereof, nor the principle of separation of church and state whenever that is part of a nation's constitution.

The quest for unity among religions is an ancient one. Current explorations in that area are only a part of that continuity. A history of the successes of such a quest would require an extensive research endeavor. Here, however, are some examples of such successes, and how they were achieved:

- Through reinterpretation of:
    a. the Bible's (Holy Bible, 1982) Old Testament, thereby absorbing Jewish ideas into Christianity, but with a different meaning.
    b. Zeno's (Fairbanks, 1898) effort at merging Jewish and Greek philosophical thought.
    c. the integration of Aristotelian logic with Christian theology.
    d. the confluence of Upanishadic, Buddhist, and Platonic thought with that of Christian theology in neo-Platonism.

- Through discussion among the leaders of various religions; for example, the inter-religious conference among Hindus, Buddhists, and Bali Aga, designed to give a cohesive form to the best elements among the three religions in Bali, was held as early as the first century A.D. at Sanyang Tiga.

- Through absorption of the ideas, belief systems, and practices of an earlier religion into a later one; examples of this abound in history, such as the:
    a. Christmas tree becoming a symbol in Christian practice.
    b. Hindu symbols and emblems in Thai Buddhism.
    c. Hindu legends and rituals absorbed into both Indonesian

and Malaysian Islam
   d. merger of the Inca and Aztec deities with saint figures in
      South American Christianity.
   e. contemporary experiments in Africa to absorb the divine,
      celestial, saintly, and/or prophetic figures of the African
      tradition into new churches and religions.
   f. Hindu songs sung with themes around Rama and
      Krishna adapted to the Muslim sentiment on occasions like
      Muharram,[1]and in the compositions of the Qavvalis, the
      Muslim bhakti (devotional) songs.

- Through understanding among neighboring individuals and societies
out of simple respect for one another; for example, Hindus distributing
sweets to:
   Muslims and vice-versa for the celebration of Eid,[2] and Muslims
   giving out sweets at occasions like Divali.[3] Two examples in
   2003 are:
   a. an Iftar[4] dinner given to Muslim leaders and divines by
      the mahant (Hindu pontiff) of the Hanuman-garhi temple,
      heretofore deeply involved in the Babri Masjid agitation in
      Ayodhya,
   b. and then a few days later, the Hanuman worship and
      recitation of Hanuman-chalisa[5] at the Eid celebration in the
      Shah Alamgir Masjid.

- Through reverence for sanctity that is innate and almost instinctive
wherever it may be found, such as:
   a. Hindus worshipping at the Dargahs[6] of the Muslim saints, for
      example, Ajmer Shareef in India.
   b. Muslims of Syria paying homage to the holy men of the
      Coptic tradition—a common phenomenon even today.
   c. reverence equally accorded by the Hindus and Muslims to
      saints like Kabir and the original Sai Baba of Shirdi.

Many other such processes of the development of conviviality and mutual absorption need to be researched in world history, recognizing the fact that these did not take place out of any form of fear, but from the natural human urge toward amity and reverence.

One of the strongest bonds of unity among religions occurs when the contemplatives of the various different streams compare notes of the experience of divine silence. In such silence, all doctrinal verbosity ceases and only a vast, interior, all-engulfing peace prevails.

The archetypes in the universal consciousness manifest themselves in numerous identical ways and forms in all the religious traditions. Again, a few examples of these parallel experiences are cited here:

- Towering prophetic figures and founders of all religions. These include the:
  a. individual founders of a religion, such as Zarathushtra the founder of the Mazdayasnians,[7] and Hazrat Muhammad, the founder of Islam.
  b. groups of founders, such as the lineages of rishis and divine incarnations (avataras) in Hinduism.
  c. prophets of the Jewish lineage, such as Abraham, Moses, and their descendents.
  d. tirthankaras[8] of the Jaina tradition.
  e. chain of Buddhas in both the northern and southern versions of Buddhism.
  f. ten gurus of the Sikh faith.

- The tradition of reading about and reciting aloud the lives of founders and great sages of the religion.

- Each religion's faith in the processes of divine revelations and the resulting sacred books.

- Sacred words, phrases, sentences, verses, and texts that may be memorized and recited repeatedly.

- The sanctity of energized spaces and waters, whether natural phenomena such as mountains, holy rivers, and streams, or special edifices.

- Sacred music and chants.

- Prayer and liturgies. The forms and wording may differ, but the fact of prayer remains, even in religions that do not believe in a creator God.

- Body positions for prayer, such as sitting in a certain way or kneeling or standing, with hands open to heaven.

- Mudras—gestures and positions of the face, hands, and body parts as manifest in the divine and sacred figures:
  a. Many of the mudras of Christ, Buddha, and the Hindu avataras are the same.
  b. The same is true for those of the Virgin Mary, many Hindu Mother Deities, and Kuang Ying.

- The importance of a divine name. One begins in:
  a. Islam "with the name of Allah."
  b. the Zarathushtrian tradition with "Pa name yazdan Hormazd khuda-e."
  c. Christianity with "In the name of the Father, the Son, and the Holy Ghost."

In the Atharva Veda (Atharvaveda Samhita, 1986), we find: "One performs the sacrifice of the Name, by the Name."

- The practice of starting a letter, a book, or any endeavor by writing the Name of God. The exhortations to remember the Name of God in every breath. Glorifying the Name of God, or of a divine figure where no creator God is accepted, in stories, legends, rituals, songs, and prayers. In contemporary Hinduism, "receiving a Name" is synonymous with initiation into a mantra—a Name of God assigned by the spiritual guide for constant recitation and meditation.

- The sanctity of transitions in life cycles and annual cycles, observed and celebrated through sacraments. Many of these celebrations sanctify identical transitions, such as birth, baptism, confirmation, marriage, and funerals, in different forms, The Jewish bar mitzvah, Vedic upanayana, and Zarathushtrian navjot all mark the transition of a youth into a life of moral responsibility and right of access to the sacred texts.[9] The celebration of seasonal cycles, sacred months, and sacred days in the annual cycle constitute worldwide festivals. These are just a few indications of a rich and wide religious diversity to be cherished and preserved, for it unites us in spirit.

- Dietary laws include:
  a. prohibitions on killing certain animals, whether because disposing of their bodies can pollute or because they are sacred.
  b. meatless days, whether through a belief in the sanctity of the universal life force, presence of a soul in all bodies, an expression of compassion for other living beings, or simply as an act of penitence, self-control, or asceticism.

- Sanctity of marriage.

- Fasting, in varying degrees.

- Practice of celibacy, if not as a permanent vow, then during certain times of the life cycle and the annual cycle, for example:
  a. exaltations to the practice of brahmacharya until marriage in the Vedic tradition.
  b. during certain nights of the month, on sacred days, and during pilgrimages.
  c. for monks and priests in various traditions.
  d. prohibition on being ham-bistar (sharing a bed) during the holy month of Ramzan, as well as during a Haj pilgrimage.

- Disciplines of clothing:
  a. special habits or garments for priests and monks.

b. head coverings for nuns in general, and for lay women when attending mass in certain Christian traditions.

c. for Jewish women when in the synagogue.

d. taking off one's hat or shoes as a mark of reverence for sacred ground.

e. other rules of modesty of clothing in the church, temple, and mosque.

- Stories of temptation and the conquest thereof:
  a. the temptation of Nachiketas in the Vedic tradition.
  b. of Zarathushtra after ten years in his cave.
  c. of the Buddha during the 49 days under the Bodhi Tree.
  d. of Jesus after the 40 days of seclusion.
  e. the story of Shiva's cosmic temptation by Kamadeva, god of desire, during the former's perennial samadhi.[10]
  f. the burning of Kamadeva, the god of love, to ashes through the beam of light emanating from Shiva's third eye.

- Periods of seclusion for 40 days of special spiritual endeavors, such as practices of prayer, penitence, and self-purification:
  a. 40 days of Lent.
  b. 40 days of the celebration of nativity in the Greek Orthodox Church.
  c. 40 days of the consecration of the Spring season in India.
  d. 40 days of chilla, the Sufi practice of withdrawing into a place of solitude for intense and incessant ascetic effort, whether in a chilla-khana, a cave, a forest, or a desert hermitage, or any other solitary place.

- Belief in a future redeemer:
  a. The return of the founder of one's own religion, as in the case of Jesus.
  b. any other messiah, as in the Jewish tradition.
  c. the future Buddha, Maitreya, in the Buddhist tradition.
  d. the Kalki Avatara, the Divine Incarnation-to-be in Hinduism.

e. in Zoroastrianism, the awaited figure of Sraoshyanta.
- Belief in the transformation of the earthly existence or the earthly city into a heavenly one, such as Jerusalem, Kashi, or Goloka.[11]

- Exhortations and commandments to:
    a. conquer human weaknesses, such as anger, jealousy, malice, violence, and greed.
    b. conquer desires.
    c. follow principles of ethics based on self-conquest, and, within that context, to conquer flesh in all forms.

- Priestly and monastic orders. Similarities of rules for various monastic, celibate, or virginal orders, such as the:
    a. rules for the Vestal Virgins.
    b. virgin guides of the community in American Indian traditions.
    c. Oneida in the African Voudou and other sacred traditions.
    d. institution of Kumari in Hinduism, especially in Nepal.
    e. similarity of the rules of St. Benedict to earlier rules for monks in the Buddhist and, yet even more ancient, Vedic renunciate orders of swamis.

- The crucial belief that the human being exists in order to elevate him/herself through great diligence toward spiritual liberation and heavenly consciousness.

- Faith in divine Grace, whether flowing directly from God or through a savior, incarnation, prophet, or Guru, or from an Enlightened One without having a belief in God.

These are only a few examples of the parallels that stand out among all religions, whether these examples were revealed independently of one another or emerged in a process of mutual borrowing or accommodation due to a spiritual urge for peaceful coexistence that was shared among the religious communities involved.

These parallels represent unifying streams that have historically played a central role in bringing about times of peaceful coexistence among religions. All of these areas call for extensive research, so that contemporary society, with the many problems that it is currently facing, may learn from history "what has been right with the world."

This perspective is not meant as support for vague, general statements such as "all religions are one." While sharing the similarities cited above, various religions maintain their own doctrinal systems that do not necessarily share a world-view or vision/perception of the divine.

Collectively encompassing the broad range of humanity's religious experience, religious systems can be divided into at least four major kinds or categories:

• Zarathushtrian, that has loaned many fundamental ideas to all religions of the world.

• Abrahamic religions of Judaism, Christianity, and Islam.

• Indian religions such as Vedic-Tamil-Hindu, Buddhist, Jain, Santa-mata, the Sikh tradition, and numerous others.

• Indigenous religions on all continents are often dismissed as animistic or nature religions because the depth of their philosophy has not been understood. This is due simply to the fact that their followers are economically disadvantaged and not articulate in the modern terminologies of the world's more dominant religions. From Australia through Africa and all of the Americas there runs a common stream of deep reverence for the presence of the divine in all phenomena. This expresses itself in an uncountable variety of beliefs, doctrines, songs, stories, epics, rituals, and in daily undertakings and interactions.

The Abrahamic religions may differ from each other on important points of doctrine, such as their views on the role of the prophet and the messiah, and yet they share a certain world view that includes:

47

- strict monotheism (note that in Christianity God is triune).
- God "created" the world, compared to the oriental cyclical view.

- the genealogy from Adam through Abraham and Moses.

- an insistence on there being only one true doctrine, and that the believers of other views are to be condemned or converted.

- only one birth for a soul, without a notion of reincarnation or a doctrine of karma

- a one-time judgment regarding whether one goes to heaven or hell (not an ongoing process).

- no incarnation or manifestation of God.

- a linear view of time.

When the parallels and similarities are examined, as well as the experience of peaceful coexistence in vast areas of human history, why is there such dissension and violence of thought (with thought being first), word, and deed among the adherents of these faiths? A close look at the universal phenomena shows that only a very subtle, slim line separates the positive from the negative, or prevents the positive energies from flowing in negative directions. Thus it is that distortions occur in the original message of love, tolerance, and peace. These distortions can include the following:

- Faith turning into an unbounded and uncontrollable devotion that manifests itself in ecstatic song or dance or, on the other hand, into a fury of fanaticism.

- In almost all religions, we read passages such as "I am savior." These passages are written in languages where the definite article "the" is not known, as is the case with Aramaic. This is one single word that has caused an immeasurable amount of strife and suffering. We fail to reconcile the saying of Jesus "I am the Way," with Krishna's statement "I am the Way." We fail to imagine that the same God has spoken through different embodiments of His own at different time periods, to different ones of his chosen people.

Thus, mixing the human weaknesses of anger, narrowness, and intolerance with readings of scripture, the adherents of each faith thereby misinterpret scripture as an exaltation of exclusivity.

Often scriptures are not read in the original but as translations of translations. A church member does not know what might have been the intent behind the words of Jesus in Aramaic translated into Hebrew or Greek or Latin or 16th century English or 21st century American. How many layers of obscuring dust have been laid upon the original meaning? Very easily the mental association with a word like "apocalyptic" suggests that the Book of Apocalypse (Holy Bible, 1982) has to do with a destructive process rather than the removal of a veil, an unveiling, which is the original intent.

As a religion spreads, in spite of its attempts to claim purity, it picks up the ideas and thoughts originally held by the people who became converts. Often it enriches the religion, as the Tamil and Balinese traditions enriched Hindu thought of Vedic origin; Celts, Druids, and Nordics enriched Christianity; and the Persian tradition, including its rich Zoroastrian content, enriched Arabia-born Islam.

Some of the prejudices of those newly converted cultures also creep in and eclipse the original meaning. It is like different peoples claiming to be racially pure, but none are proved to be so upon examination of their genetic inheritance. It is now no longer possible to eradicate genes inherited from the millennia of racial mix; so also it is not possible to separate the original from the accretions in any religion. The efforts at doing so are not only self-defeating, they are also destructive as, for example, the attempts of some elements of contemporary Islam to "purify" Malay and Indonesian Islam by eliminating all that was preserved there from previous cultural traditions.

Often religions have become identified with ethnic groups and nations. This happens in many ways:

• Certain ethnic groups are inheritors of a revelation and, thereby, have a claim to being God's chosen people. This is the situation with the Jewish faith. Here, faith and ethnicity appear to be inseparable, but, seeing a wide variety of racial types, languages, and customs, one may question whether the Jews are truly as exclusive in the matter of the ethnicity-religion amalgam as they appear to be. If they could separate conflicts with other ethnic groups from conflicts with other religions, and analyze the contents of the two separately, this may very well prove conducive to peace.

• Some ethnic groups that actively attempt to preserve a religion neither attempt to convert others nor accept converts from the outside. Their religion and ethnicity have been historically one, even though their scriptures may be mute on the matter, as is true with the Zoroastrians. It would not be a simple matter to separate ethnicity from religion in such a case. Integration of the two in such groups may be acceptable only if they continue to maintain their neutrality and amity toward other religions as they have done throughout their history.

• A group of people, for example, in an African territory, accepts the tenets of Islam while another group accepts Christianity. The two are traditional enemies who have perpetrated acts of cruelty upon each other for quite some time. That cruelty then became attributed to the religion that they had recently adopted, so it is now perceived that Christians are killing Muslims or Muslims are killing Christians. What is actually happening in this case, however, is that one tribal-minded group is killing another tribal-minded group that now happens to have adopted a different religion. This has been the case in the conflict between the Serbs and the Cosovars. In addition, scripture has often been used to justify the oppression of one people by another, as when certain Christian churches attempted to justify apartheid in South Africa.

• Often the strife among nations manifests itself as an attack on the religion of the defeated and weaker. An event of this nature that occurred many centuries ago is viewed today as an act of religious persecution, whereas it was, by and large, a conqueror's attempt to destroy the identity of a certain people, as in the case of Alexander destroying the Zarathustrian fire temples and burning their holy books. Could the "guru" of Alexander of Macedonia, Aristotle the philosopher, have actually ordered his disciple to destroy such great works of philosophy as the Gathas (Faiss & Humbach, 2010)[12] and the Avesta (Geldner, 1986) of the Mazdayasnians? Yet, the fact of destruction remains, the main purpose of which was the political subjugation of a nation by vengefully destroying its identity. This is most easily achieved through the suppression and desecration of its religion.

The propagandists of different religions have the age-old habit of:

• choosing the best and most inspiring passages from their own texts and the most creative and beautiful periods of their history, while, at the same time,

• selecting the worst passages and periods of history from the adherents of an opposite religion, and then comparing the two.

In return, those they oppose use the same tool, citing the best examples from their own scriptures and history while attacking those of their opponents.

Why not, instead, admit to ourselves our own failures, and erase from our consciousness all that is destructive in our understanding of our own doctrines and history?

The age-old enmities among nations, easily identified with the religions that they followed, cultivated, and perpetuated both an imperial complex (e.g., "we are their rulers") and a persecution complex. Those who perceived themselves to have been persecuted become free, and then justify their own vendetta against their erstwhile rulers. In this way, the cycle of mutual destruction continues.

In a similar way, a nostalgia for an imagined history often follows: "we were so great," "our boundaries once extended a hundred thousand miles in each direction; oh, my, how we have shrunk!" If people of a certain nation-religion (where nation and religion are confused with one another) ruled over an area for a relatively brief period of history, they continue to claim those areas as parts of their national-religious boundaries, and their psyche continues to strive to regain that lost power and glory by means of hate and destruction.

Religion is often used for purely mundane purposes. This has prevailed in the history of Europe, as well as in the histories of other continents. To cite a few examples:

- looting the vanquished so that the temple/cathedral/mosque of the conqueror would be enriched. The gold of the Incas and Aztecs, who were mercilessly killed, was used to build some of the great Cathedrals of Europe;

- preachers exhorting the exploited workers to accept the extremes of their work, and not to protest that their young children were working sixteen hours a day in the coal mines and other industries (as was the case up to the end of the 19th century, and even in many countries today);

- some orthodox Hindu preachers misinterpreting and misapplying the karma doctrine in order to justify the gross exploitation of the "lesser" castes;

- priests who were bound by allegiance to the secular heroes/kings/commanders/presidents saying and doing whatever was expected of them by the donor and/or the patron.

Without a complete personal purification of the priest and the preacher, this trend will not stop, and the continued misuse of religion for ethnic, national, political, and economic purposes will continue.

Those who have chosen the false identities of nation and religion have been the cause of much suffering for humanity. Priests in each country pray for the victory of their countrymen and not for the people of vanquished lands and nations, even though they are of the same religion. We live in a world where ideals are cherished, so that, in the Anglo-French wars, for example, the Anglican priest as a man of God should be as concerned for the loss of French lives as he grieves over the loss of English ones, but the French priest prays for France and the English priest prays for England. And, if the French happen to be Roman Catholics, well then, it is understood that they stand no chance of entering heaven as far as the Anglican priest is concerned!

The only way out of this dilemma is to define religion as separate from ethnicity, nation, state, or political groupings. Unfortunately, even in countries where the separation of religion and state is a fundamental principle of the declared polity, the total separation has never really occurred because the minds of the people have not changed. With the tacit approval of the society's political system, some pulpits continue to serve as avengers and not redeemers of the sinfully "wicked."

This is the darker side of the human mind that stands in contrast to its brighter side, as evidenced by the numerous examples cited above. It is the strength and purity manifest in those examples that would help divest religion of all its negative accretions. In adopting these qualities, religion would then serve as only a source of inspiration for nonviolence and love.

Those pure enough to have stepped out of these false identities that have been imposed upon religion are the reformers and renunciates of history who were often persecuted. A careful study of these instances will show that most often those who have divested themselves of such false identities associated with religion have been the contemplatives. They each found their revelation in moments of experiencing the mystery while traveling a path of self-examination, andself-purification, and in some cases, having a direct experience of God.

The contemplatives and great thinkers—who have understood that the origin of every religion lies in some profound and unique internal experience of divinity—pursued that experience with great diligence and ascetic endeavor, eventually becoming a founder. It is in a state of such unique and profound consciousness that all revelations have occurred. For this reason, in all continents and among all peoples, those who seek spiritual truth wander off into short or long periods of silence and solitude (khalwa in Sufi; ekanta in Sanskrit) that could be forty days or ten years in duration. Once we have found this source of religion in higher levels of consciousness, we would not venture into sullying the teachings that arise from this source; we would attempt to maintain its purity and, if possible, to replicate the experience. This is the basis of the experiments and methods on the mystic path that the founders of all religions have pursued.

Thus it is the revival of the contemplative and meditative path that will bring people back to their rightful inheritance—the pure core of spiritual experience. Only in this way will we prevent a repeat of the destruction that the false identities imposed on religion have wrought.

In other words, the unity of religions is to be found in the likes of the dervesh, the pir, the mendicant, and the wandering sadhu. It is they, who from all different religions in the past, gathered together around a fire in the courtyard of a wayside inn or hermit's hut and spoke about their plunge into divinity, often sharing it in a group silence. These were the true inter-religious conferences, the effects of which can be seen in the thread of unity and parallel expressions in rituals among all peoples of the world. To strengthen the thread of unity among all religions, we must strive for unification of the individual soul with the Supreme Consciousness, whether we call this God, name it bodhi, or, better still, as in the Tao and in the Upanishads (Ekadasopanisadah, 1966; Hume, 1971), leave it as Nameless.

It is to achieve this union with God—that would then unite the spiritual guides of various faiths—that the contemplatives of all traditions went off to dwell in solitary caves. We read in the ancient Rig Veda (Kashyap, 2003):

> In the cave of the mountains,
> at the confluences of the rivers,
> one becomes wise by meditation.
> RIG VEDA (8.6.28)

Zarathushtra communed with the divine fire in a cave for ten years to receive the revelations bestowed by Ahura Mazda. Jesus was born in a grotto, and later ascended to heaven from a cave. The cave of St. Francis of Assisi still, to this day, invokes a presence of peace in the pilgrim. Hazrat Mohammad often withdrew to the cave of Hira where revelation of parts of the Qu'ran occurred. The great yogis still dwell in the Himalayan caves, as do the contemplative Coptic monks who do not leave the underground caves of their monasteries in Ethiopia for many years at a time, as well as the contemplative monks of Mount Athos in Greece. Above all, as the Upanishads say, is the Cave of the Heart that the contemplative has learned to enter for true solitude. This one can do whether one is a cobbler sitting on a city street, a commander in the battlefield, or a computer expert in the information technology industry.

What do these unifiers of the human soul with God, and consequently the unifiers of humanity, do in these caves of contemplation? They undertake the practices of silence, fasting, celibacy, prayer, rosary, and penitence, as well as changing the position of their mind by experimenting with positions of their body. The disciplines practiced in periods of solitude cannot always be revealed to the uninitiated, lest they cause harm. Some of these practices, however, can be undertaken by anyone whether he/she be a recluse or a lay person.

From the vast repertoire of meditative methodologies known in the Sino-Indian traditions (e.g., Dhyana-yoga, Jhana, Ch'an, Son, and Zen),[13] let us look at a few that are practiced in common by different religions. The extent of sophistication in the variety of methods may differ, but many principles of contemplative and meditative practices are shared by the adherents of different faiths and religions. An understanding of these will lead us to a core experience that cannot fail to unite us, even if different doctrines are followed and various world views are held. Only when one reaches the pinnacle of the direct personal experience of the Divine can one truly comprehend the original meaning of the scriptures that recorded the founder's own inner ecstasy and revelation.

Quite often teachers of the philosophies of meditation are misunderstood as propounding a religion—their religion. This misunderstanding occurs because the revelation, the unveiling of reality in consciousness, has occurred in the deepest possible contemplative state, which was then misinterpreted by followers of the religion who themselves had no personal revelation and were in no position to convey the trans-intellectual meaning of the great founder's words. As a meditator progressively derives his/her spiritual nutrition from the deeper "interior" unveiling, he/she is able to go beyond the confines of language to convey the experience of this Silence. The meaning of such a person's words often changes (in the mind of the listener) when the meditator refers to this deeper consciousness. The meditator has no other vocabulary for it. Those whose intellect thrives exclusively on the "exterior" can only hear in such words what they themselves mean by those words. In Silence, there are no theologies, no taxonomies. An atheist can equally experience this silence through meditative methods, and in that silence will eventually come upon the Nameless One. When speaking of that One, however, others will still think that person is teaching religion!

Contemplation and Meditation

Here are some of the many practices of contemplation and meditation that are common to the major religions. They can be described here only briefly. The detailed practices may take decades to bear fruit, or results may appear instantly, depending on the practitioner's level of internal purification.

Remembering the Name

One practice is traditionally known as nama-smarana, remembering the Divine Names. Such remembrance is called japa in Sanskrit. In the Sikh Guru Granth Sahib (Singh, 1989; Veda Bharati, 1998),[14] we read:

Hari hari namu japu prana adharu...
Rama nama japi ekankaru

Do the japa of the Name
"Oh Divine One, Oh Divine One" thus.
Do the recitation of the Name
of the "Delightful One" [for He is the], One Om.

Different religions and languages have different names for Divinity. The Hindus recite 1,008 names, each a different manifestation of divinity. In Islam, there are 99 that are commonly known.

There are many ways of remembering the Name: singing aloud, reciting, mumbling, and thinking the Name in the mind and heart that then becomes meditation.

A guru, a pir, or a spiritual director may assign a particular name for a disciple to recite constantly, with or without a rosary. The higher the spiritual status of the guide, the deeper in the mind, without vocalization, the disciple's experience of the Name will be. The disciple approaches the spiritual director with a request to confer a Divine Name for recitation and constant remembrance, and promises to him/herself to always keep it in his/her heart. As we read in the Guru Granth Sahib:

Nanaka dijay nama dana
Rakhau hiye paroyee

Nanak [begs]: grant [me] the Name;
I shall keep it strung in the heart.

Thus, a Divine Name may often be used as a mantra, either alone or in combination with other syllables and words. If you have an objection to the word "mantra," call it a one-word prayer in silence, as we read in the classic Cloud of Unknowing (Baker & McCann, 1952). As the meditation dives deeper, the remembrance of the Name becomes natural, and deeply interiorized.

Such a name, taken into the depths of one's consciousness, releases powerful purifying energies, and generates internal celestial music. The sound of the sacred syllable, the secret of the mantra science, brings one face-to-face with one's Beloved God. In the Guru Granth Sahib:

akhara nada kathana bakhiana...
drisatiman akhara hai jeta
nanaka parabrahma niralepa

[How is one to] narrate a description of the sound of
the Indestructible Syllable?
One who has found the vision of the Syllable,
says Nanak, [has found] the unsmearable
transcendental Brahman.

Here it should be remembered that one is advised to restrain one's vocalizations. The texts, such as the Guru Granth Sahib, do not say "repeat the name," but rather:

Nanaka nama dhiayiye sacchi badiyayi

Says Nanak, meditate on the name and
that is true greatness.

Contemplation

The Vedantic manana means contemplating the meaning of a metaphysical phrase or a word from the scriptures until the meaning becomes a reality to oneself.

In the Christian tradition, one may choose, or be given by one's spiritual director, a particular passage from the Bible, whether a line from a Psalm or a saying of Jesus, to read, ponder, and apply to one's deeper self in order to achieve a transformation within or to experience a closeness to God.

Similarly, the Sufi novitiate is given a phrase from the Qur'an (Ali, 1995; Maududi, 1996), the kalam Allah, that is "revealed to humanity wrapped in many thousands of veils." The murid, or disciple, contemplates a passage assigned by his pir until he/she ceases to be "dar wujud," in body, and has achieved the nafs-e-haqiqat-e-khud, the essence of the reality of self.

Those in the traditions of yoga meditation (belonging to whichever religious denomination of Indian origin) are given similar passages from the Vedic, Buddhist, Jain, Sikh, or other traditions. The same applies to the Mazdayasnian tradition. The system of contemplation in the traditions of India is most refined in the Vedanta path. Every novitiate is given a maha-vakya, a Great Sentence, because of its depth of meaning. There are four main maha-vakyas in Vedanta, but in other associated traditions, one may choose from over a hundred. For example, the maha-vakya "tat tvam asi," "That Thou Art," may take an entire lifetime to unravel internally. The Gur-mantar of the Sikhs, the five nama-karas of the Jainas, and so forth—together with additional passages from the respective scriptures—may be presented to the mind to contemplate.

In all of these systems, there are parallel methodologies of using internalized logic that constitutes manana, contemplation (uha in the Yoga Sutras of Patanjali [Hariharananda Aranya, 1983], tarka in the Tantric systems), the most essential part of internal dialogue. Until one has completely assimilated the innermost meaning of such a word, phrase, or passage, a self-transformation has not been completed. The assigned passage remains the object of contemplation day and night. So it is among the Sufis, Vedantins, and yogis.

Riddles

Mutually contradictory or "impossible" statements are used by numerous meditative traditions as passages for contemplation. The purpose is to take the mind beyond common logic, and to bring opposite concepts into a transcendent unification. One may be required to unravel the riddle until a spiritual breakthrough and transformation of consciousness has occurred. This practice is true of all contemplative systems.

How does one spiritually reconcile these seemingly inconsistent and opposing statements?

"There is a God." "There is no God."
"There is a self." "There is no self."

How does one begin to understand Kabir when he sings of:

The ant that carries away an elephant,
or the Koan,
The shore (or the bridge) flowed;
The river stood still.

Sometimes I went to my Master with a simple question about practical matters, asking:
"Should I do it this way, or that way?"

And his reply would come in a deep voice arising out of the heart:
"Yeeeessss, indeeeed."

I was meant to unravel such a reply. And what is the meaning of Jesus saying:

"Before Abraham was, I am."

Body Posture

Training oneself to assume a certain position for prayer, contemplation, and self-conquest is a common method in all religions. The sequence of various body positions in the course of namaz or salat[15] is an example of the same.

In Christianity, when praying while sitting on a hard bench, kneeling, or standing, one becomes so absorbed in prayer and meditation that any body discomfort is forgotten. The stories of Christian saints remaining in the same position in prayer throughout the night are legendary. Traditions of India, like yoga, are the most sophisticated and detailed in this regard, the Jain kayotsarga practices being the foremost. The Sufi training is not too far behind. The same applies to mudras, the hand positions in Christian or Muslim prayer. Indian traditions teach hundreds of such mudras for different types and stages of prayer and worship.

Ambulatory Prayer

Prayer while walking is one of the common practices among the followers of many religions. A Christian, Buddhist, or a Hindu monk keeps turning the beads of the rosary or mala while walking. It is an inspiring sight to see the Turkish lay people walking the streets of German cities while practicing their tasbeeh. In a recent meeting with a delegation of the World Council of Religious Leaders, the prime minister of Palestine appeared with his rosary in hand. And the Tibetan walks everywhere with a prayer wheel.

One common example of ambulatory prayer is the religious procession or circumambulation at holy sites, sacred cities, and edifices, with or without prescribed rituals, practiced in all religions. Such prayerful practices are also an essential part of pilgrimages in these same religions.

The deepest practice of ambulatory prayer is contemplative walking that is taught in most Buddhist and Swamis' monasteries, in Sufi khanqahs,[16] and in the Zen-dos. It is often practiced by Christian monks as well. One walks to and fro within the confines of parallel lines of suitable length, or in a limited area of the monastery, or within a pattern or vyu-ha, such as a labyrinth. The detailed internal system of the contemplative walk is taught by the masters of various traditions.

Confession

Internal dialogue for self-purification and surrender is one of the core practices in the contemplative method. One examines one's weaknesses, argues pro and con, counters any tendency to "giving excuses," confesses to oneself, and renews the vow for self-purification, to free oneself from any gunah, sin, or zillat (i.e., a "slip.") Slowly one recognizes and then fills any remaining gaps between oneself and God. Christians confess to their sinfulness, while the Hindus recite, "papo'ham,"[17] seeking to cleanse themselves of the transgressions committed in the day or night with thought, word, or deed. In the words of the Veda (e.g., Macdonell, Muller, & Oldenberg, 2005):

Yad-ahna papam-akarsham…
Yad ratrya papam akarsham…
Manasa vacha karmana…

What transgressions I have committed by the day…
What transgressions I have committed by the night…
With mind, speech, and act…

So the Mazdayasnian in the liturgies of Khurd-Avesta (e.g., Geldner, 1986):[18]

Az an gunah manashni gavashni kunashni,
Tani ravani, geti minoani, okhe awakhsh pasheman pa se
Gavashni pa patet hom… Kshaothra ahurahe mazda

I renounce all wrong thoughts, wrong words, and wrong deeds
I have committed, that have occurred through me, have been
originated by me.

All transgressions I have committed in thought, word, and deed, through body, speech, and mind - I herewith renounce.
So may the Great Lord redeem me.

Without such recognition of inner impurities, one cannot progress to the ideal of evoking the presence of the divine in the earthly realm.
Such confession then leads to acts of penitence or prayashchitta, not only for transgressions committed, but the duties and acts of love, service, and devotion omitted. In Vedic liturgy:

Kim aham papam akaravam
Kim aham sadhu nakaravam

What transgressions I have committed;
What right acts I have omitted.

In Islam, without repentance (tawba) there can be no sainthood.
In this context of speaking in a contemplative way to one's own mind, Indian saints wrote many songs addressed to the mind's self-purification, so that pilgrims would not be waylayed on their path to God. In the Guru Granth Sahib:

Karahale mana pardesiya...
Mana karahala sati guru purakhu dhiyai...

O Mind, O exile,
O Mind, meditate upon the true guru,
the Transcendent Person.

One prays for the removal of all signs and stains of ego and anger from the mind, so that the mind may become a fit vehicle to lead one to God
In the Guru Granth Sahib:

Jaba ihu mana mahi karata gumana;

Taba ihu bavaru phirata bigana.

When one allows egoism in the mind,
It is then the mind wanders, a lost, crazy stranger.

Visualizations

Many different forms of visualizations, done with devotion and surrender, are practiced as part of the contemplative and meditative systems of various faiths.

A Christian may visualize the suffering of Christ in the Stations of the Cross, His compassionate visage, the Pieta figure, or the mental image of a saint. This may be accompanied with contemplations of sacred phrases as described above.

In Hindu liturgy, the very first act is the mental recitation of the dhyana-shloka, a verse that actively invites a visualization that is held in meditation, not merely invoking the presence of the Divinity but "seeing" the divine presence in the mind's eye in precise iconographic detail.

The most elaborate visualizations are taught in the Tibetan tradition.

The practice of visualization as a system of meditation is elaborate and shared by many traditions. Images repeatedly imprinted upon the mind lead to:

- an internal transformation

- revelation of the true nature of the chosen form of one's Deity

- eventual identification with the divine figure so that the attributes of the Divine descend into the very soul of the devotee.

One form of visualization is a concentration on the image of a written word or symbol, such as the sign of Om, the Arabic form of "Allah," a svastika,[19] the cross in its many versions, and even the chosen Name or mantra written and visualized in its native script. A Sufi may visualize the very first nuqteh or bindu,[20] the dot under the Arabic letter "bay" (letter "B") with which the Qur'an begins. Or one may visualize the same dot on

63

top of the sign for Om. Through this literally one-pointed concentration, one may enter the gateway to infinity.

Some visualizations are practiced in the heart, at the forehead, or in other centers, together with many different variations and/or embellishments.

Identification

In the Bhagavad Gita (Radhakrishnan, 1948; Shankaracarya, 1977):

yo yach-chraddhah sa eva sah

Whatever one dwells upon that verily does one become.
Bhagavad Gita (17.3)

When one visualizes one's chosen form of divinity, together with the appropriate Name, mantra, or prayer, and it becomes a constant baseline thought and "feeling" within oneself, the transformation that occurs produces a sense of identity with the Beloved One. Those who keep the Deity in their hearts and minds begin to exhibit traits similar to the object of their worship. The Buddhist develops the Buddha-like mien and mudra, the Sufi seeks to become like Ali and Ishmael, and the Christian may experience the stigmata. At that point, it is difficult to draw the line between the consciousness of the devotee and the consciousness of the Deity. When the Vedantic affirmation tat tvam asi ("that thou art") is applied to bhakti-yoga in this relationship, one states oneself to be "That"— so'ham ("I am That") or shivo'ham ("I am Shiva"); ana anta wa-anta ana says the Sufi ("I am you and you are I.")

This seeking of some degree of identification (e.g., to become Christlike or Buddha-like) is common to all religions.

Breathing

The meditative practice most commonly shared by various religions is that of prayer with an awareness of breath. This takes many simple or progressively complex forms. Let each breath become a prayer — this is an exhortation to all devotees of all religions.

The awareness of breath flow is a primary ingredient of meditation and is part of the practice of mindfulness (sati-patthana in Buddhism, smrty-upa-sthana in the Yoga Sutras of Patanjali).

In the vipassana[21] system, no particular prayer word is permitted. I, however, have met Thai monks in the Sukhothai forest who use a name of the Buddha in its Pali language version, buddho. In Northern Buddhism, as in the yoga tradition, the use of a short mantra in synchrony with the breath is a common practice. Similar practices are included in the Jain meditative tradition of preksha-dhyana.[22]

One learns to breathe diaphragmatically, breathing slowly, gently, and without a jerk or sound in the breath, while feeling the flow and touch of the breath in the nostrils. One keeps the mantra or the prayer word flowing in the mind, while sensing and observing the gentle flow of the breath.

This practice has many variations that are prescribed by the meditation guide to students with different capacities and psycho-spiritual personality profiles. Examples include observing the breath flow from the navel while letting the word also flow, or remembering the word in the cavity of the heart.

Buddhist and yoga breath meditation practices have identical parallels in the Sufi practice of Zikr (Dhikr).[23] Christian meditative traditions such as hesychia[24] include the exact same methods. Even St. Ignatius of Loyola (Ganss, 1991) includes prayer with breath rhythms in his Spiritual Exercises.

We read in the Sikh scripture, the Guru Granth Sahib:

Sasi sasi aradhe niramala soi janu

Only one who worships in every breath becomes a pure person.

The practices of prayer and meditation with breath awareness are the ones most commonly shared among various religions.

Silence as Common Prayer

In inter-religious gatherings, it has been a common practice for the guides of different faiths to lead a prayer, each according to his/her own tradition. The true unity of prayer, however, occurs in silence. Even though it is customary to take a minute or two of silence to mark special events, the mind's practice of true meditative and contemplative silence is rare.

Only minds that are at peace can deliberate on ways of finding peace among societies. Minds that are not harmonized within cannot bring harmony in the external world of relationships.

It would be ideal if, wherever there are people of different faiths, languages, and/or nationalities gathered together, they would begin and end their deliberations by entering a deep state of silence through the practice of a prayer recited with each and every breath. The efficacy of this practice for bringing a sense of unity and a feeling of peace can be demonstrated universally in no more than five minutes of a silence guided by one who is proficient in meditation.

Atheist's Meditation

An objection may be raised to such a "method of prayerful silence" by those who do not believe in any form of prayer. Even then, meditation practices that do not use a prayer or sacred phrase can be easily shown to effect a peaceful state of mind. This has been demonstrated in numerous medical and scientific experiments. It is indeed possible to meditate without having a belief in God or using prayer by following the same method of breath awareness described above and simply counting the breaths. Again, there are many ways and permutations of doing this count that can be learned from an authentic teacher.

Consider one additional question. How many of the presently existing religions are being truly represented at the so-called global inter-religious gatherings?

Those economically disadvantaged, as well as those that are not very articulate in modern terminologies, have no influence on the deliberations and decision-making processes. Only the "great religions of the world" have a voice.

What distinguishes the "great religions" from the "not-so-great" ones? Is it the economic or political power? Is it contemporary influence through that power? What does that have to do with true spirituality? Is it the number of adherents? Who are we to say that because an idea is upheld by a large number of people, that this alone constitutes its greatness as an idea per se?

Are we great because we are aggressive conquerors who have decimated the numbers, power, and strength of the weaker vanquished ones, and use that power mongering as an argument in favor of our greatness? Is it not true that in the eyes of God, it is the meek that are truly great?

Considering the ways in which the greatness of a religion is viewed and weighed, would Shinto be included among the "great religions" of the world had Japan by chance won the Second World War? Would Voudou be a "great religion" if its devotees had not been colonized and enslaved, or if they had developed some substantial economic power?

In the view of a silent meditator, a religion is great not on these grounds but because it has influenced humanity throughout its history in a selfless and beneficial way, and has given birth and impetus to the arts, sciences, and peaceful social structures. It is great because its ideas are philosophically sound, whether written down or simply taught orally, and those ideas have lead to the spiritual elevation of the human mind.

Thus, the Zarathushtrian tradition with a maximum of a quarter million adherents and the Jaina faith with a few million followers, as well as some of the indigenous traditions worldwide, are just as great as the more populous religions that hold the reins of secular power and use it to prove that they are thereby great. In our endeavors for unity among religions we need to undertake, inter alia, the following measures:

• The adherents of different faiths need to resolve not to judge the value of a religion as great or small but to include all religions in their deliberations regarding whatever affects humanity at large.

• The leaders, guides, and scholars of each religion need to institute research into their own past, confessing to themselves, and then to the world, their own historical transgressions against the peoples of other faiths. Did we destroy the places of worship of any other religions? Did we use force or fraud? If so, then they need to apologize and atone for the transgressions committed. The recent apologies by the Pope offered to the Jewish people indicate the direction in which we need to move. Yet even in this instance, why were apologies not offered to the Incas as well?

Such apologies are only as a beginning. Every religion, on a global scale, has something to apologize for.

• These same leaders need to resolve and declare that to condemn the adherents of other religions or to criticize or denounce their doctrine, belief system, and practices is a violation of the principles of human rights, accepting the fact that:

    a. using abusive language and maligning anyone intentionally do not fall within the category of freedom of speech, and

    b. the condemnation of other religions is often a cause of riots, civil strife, and wars.

Rather, the teachers of religion should vow to state only their own belief systems while recognizing the beauty of those of others with reverence and in a spirit of love.

It is essential to institute research into:

• the commonalities of religious belief and spiritual experience

• the examples of mutual respect and accommodation that can be found throughout human history.

After realizing the strengths of such wisdom and love that have led to mutual conviviality and peace, spiritual leaders then need to apply those strengths, and the manners in which they were put to practice, in order to help solve contemporary problems of strife and dissension.

Educators need to prepare textbooks illustrating the commonalities of religious experience, while, at the same time, respectfully recognizing the beauty of particular beliefs that are specific to certain religions. Parents throughout the world can be encouraged to read to their children:

• selections from texts of religions insofar as they do not violate their own beliefs, and

• life stories of the saintly among all religions.

As part of peace education, religious leaders, educators, and parents must undertake the training of minds to be at peace through the practice of contemplative methods by making a spiritually oriented meditation practice as a highly recommended part of:

- life at home.

- the curriculum in educational institutions worldwide. For non believers, meditation systems that are not associated with any religion should be taught.

The leaders of all religions, as well as those of national entities, must confer among themselves to find ways to separate deeply ingrained concepts that bind the identities of ethnicity and religion.

The contemplative masters of all schools must consult in order to find ways to stop equating spirituality with religion. Spirituality must be defined as a system of values for the individual and society that includes the development of a nonviolent, tolerant, and forgiving personality, and a lifestyle of devotion and personal contemplative experience, without any prejudice or judgment of "other" systems of religion, society, culture, ethnicity, and creed.

The leaders in all spheres of life need to find ways to honor the wise and the elders of all religions equally.

May human beings learn to remember what has been harmonious and beautiful in the past, and may they recognize what is right in the present.

May we implement the lessons provided by these beautiful experiences to fill the voids of human minds, and to vanquish the miseries suffered by countless millions. May peace be translated into our earthly endeavors without, as it is experienced in the heavenly consciousness within.

CHAPTER 3
Polymorphous Monotheism

In the history of inter-religious relationships, wherever the various religions have encountered each other, there have been violent conflicts as well as dialogues for mutual understanding. We do not know what the contents of the dialogues were in the courts of Harshavardhana, Harun-al-Rashid, Changis Khan, Kublai Khan, or Akbar the Great. For the past century and a half, interfaith dialogues have been conducted with greater frequency and covering a larger scope than ever before. In these dialogues, debaters of each religion try to outdo the others by stating how the truth of their own religion is the most tolerant. No doctrinal formula seems to have been found that would help embrace the truth of all different religions. Here the key issue of monotheism versus polytheism needs to be resolved.

For many thousands of years, a bitter debate has been raging between strict monotheists and those who believe in the diverse forms of divinity. The acrimony has often been violent throughout history. The Bible's (Holy Bible, 1982) Old Testament bears testimony to such violence; the relationships between the Abrahamic and all other religions have been dictated by this difference of doctrinal perceptions. Is it at all possible to bridge such a vast chasm between religions? Is there a median place where the two views do meet?

Although this discussion is primarily centered in the history of India's religious thought, the concepts are universal and applicable to any debate between Abrahamic monotheism and others. They are equally relevant to established religions such as Hinduism and Shinto, and what are often unfairly lumped together as the "indigenous" religions in different parts of

71

Asia, Africa, and other parts of the world.

Many times during worldwide travels a Swami is asked, "What do Hindus believe? It looks like there are too many gods, too many figures. How does one keep track of them all?" In response, a simple credo may be offered from the Bhagavad Gita (Radhakrishnan, 1948; Shankaracarya, 1977):

> On whichever path men walk, they come unto Me.
> Whichever form or aspect of Mine they worship,
> towards that very form of Mine do I strengthen their faith;
> and through that faith they come unto Me.

This is a statement by God[1] incarnate as Krishna. The history of this thought may be traced back to the earliest Vedic times as in the Rig Veda (Kashyap, 2003) where God is referred to as vishu-rupa. The word "vish-va-rupa," for those who know Sanskrit, comes later. The Vedic word, "vishu-rupa" means "he of many forms." Vishu-rupa's vi-bhuti, the great Mother Force, shines in many forms, manifesting Her own many glories.

So we read in the Rig Veda:

> Eka evaagnir bahudha samidhhah
> Ekah suryo vishvam anu-pra-bhutah
> Ekaivoshaah sarvam idam vi-bhaati
> Ekam vaa idam
> vi-babhuva sarvam

> One fire burns in so many different flames;
> One sun shines as the power over all the different beings;
> One dawn makes everything shine brilliantly in all her
> different natures;
> It is but One; there is only One; this all, this variety is but One
> That has become many; has assumed multifarious forms.

Here vi-babhuva may be translated as: has become multiplied, has become manifest in his vi-bhutis. We read in the vi-bhuti chapter of the Bhagavad Gita a long list of His vi-bhutis, the glories that are the varieties in His One Being. The seed of the vi-bhuti pada of the Yoga Sutras of Patanjali (Hariharananda Aranya, 1983) elucidates the powers that may be acquired by a yogin. The verse declares how the One vi babhuva sarvam, has become this entire manifold and varied universe with all its phenomena.

In the great epic, the Mahabharata (Narasimhan, 1965), one of the longest epic poems in the world containing 100,000 verses, there are two very great characters who are master teachers. One is Krishna who, of the 100,000 verses in the epic, taught 2,200 verses, 700 of which comprise the Bhagavad Gita.

Then there is the great character named Bhishma, the grand patriarch who at the age of 145 led the army of the Kauravas for nine days. Of the 100,000 verses, 20,000 are Bhishma's teachings, constituting one-fifth of the Mahabharata. The core of that teaching is found in a portion called Bhishma-stava-raja—the "King of Hymns" by Bhishma.[2] One verse in that "King of Hymns" reads:

Yam
Prthag-dharma-charanaah
prthag-dharma-phalaishinah
prthag-dharmaih sam-archanti
tasmai dharmaatmane namah

Those who walk on the different paths of dharmas
Each seeking his own fruit of dharma
To whom they offer their worship with and through all the different dharmas, all of these different paths of belief and conduct
My homage unto that dharma-atman, one whose very self is dharma.

It is impossible to translate the word "religion" into any Indian language. Teachings of Hinduism as well as Taoism cannot be called a religion. They represent a freedom of many paths—as many paths as you choose, on whichever path you choose to walk. Those who perform worship to the Shiva form also pay homage to the Vishnu form. Those who perform worship to the Vishnu form always pay homage to the Shiva form. One of the verses often chanted in Hindu liturgy is:

> I do not know of what kind and nature Thou art;
> Of whatever kind of Deity Thou art,
> Oh Great Divine Being,
> My homage to that very kind of Thee.

So also every Taoist temple, along with the Taoist Deities, venerates the Buddha, just as the Chinese Buddhist temples have Taoist deities also. There are also many forms of the Buddha and Bodhisattvas that are venerated throughout the Mahayana Buddhist countries. Deities such as the "Hindu" Ganesha are to be found not only in India but in Buddhist Tibet and Japan as well. The Japanese of the Shinto persuasion appear to worship the many kamis, but these are all emanations of the one Amaterasu, the Mother Sun.

> Thus, God may be defined as Shunya, infinite,
> One in many, and many in One.

In fact, none of the cultures reputed to be polytheistic is truly polytheistic. Different parts of the Spirit are believed to be emanations or powers of the One, known by whatever name in the so-called indigenous languages.

This ineffable, indefinable nature of Divinity is further emphasized in a verse often recited in India:

> I do not know the Benevolent One,
> Then, how can I speak of Him;
> I do know the Benevolent One,
> Then, how can I speak of Him?

A very crucial question in the study of world religions is, as stated above: religions are often divided into two types—monotheistic and polytheistic, those who believe in one God, and those who believe in many gods. The distinction is made between god with a small "g," and God with a capital "G." This division in itself is fallacious. There can be perhaps three divisions: monotheism, polytheism, and polymorphous monotheism. Discussions of the transcendental, such as those of Kant and Emerson, and idealist monism like that of Bishop Berkley and Shankara in Vedanta, as well as the non-self doctrine of Buddhism, are not being included here.

Polymorphism here is our neologism as a translation of vishu-rupa: One God of many forms. Monotheistic religions may be divided into two categories: monomorphous monotheism and polymorphous monotheism. One God of only one form is the accepted credo in the Abrahamic religion with its three branches of Judaism, Christianity, and Islam. Other Eastern religions believe, like many of the ancient Greeks, in one God who manifests Herself or Himself in multiple forms through all the many cycles of creations and dissolutions.

Often polymorphous monotheism entails cosmology that is not temporally or spatially monolateral. It is not that God created the world once and will destroy the world. It is circles within circles, cycles within cycles, chakras, that is, multi-layered wheels of space and time. Those raised in the traditions of India are brought up reading the Upanishads (Ekadasopanisadah, 1966; Hume, 1971) and Vedic literature about ananta-koti -brahmaanda—uncountable billions of universes being created at this very time. So when someone speaks about God having created the world in some past time, which particular world is it that is being referred to? Which one of the uncountable billion universes is this sarshapa-matra,[3] that is "mere mustard-seed-size" earth? It is commonly declared to be thus in every Hindu liturgy. Within each cycle, in each historical period, in all the different continents and countries, the Divine Being manifests Itself, Himself, Herself according to the form that is needed by the people of that time, that group, that particular continent. The given manifestation reveals Her/Himself in their language and with their referents. This is polymorphous monotheism.

The believers of polymorphous monotheism worldwide are able to accommodate whichever manifestation of God the people of any other religion may worship. It is quite common in many parts of India to honor the diverse manifestations through their icons. One may even find, along with Hindu icons from all over the world, images of Jesus or Mary. Oh! Another revelation of God, how beautiful, how glorious! In the same spirit, Catholic saints are identified with the ancient Maya and Aztec deities in many parts of South America. Similar instances are to be found in many parts of Africa in cross identification between the Voudou, Orixa, and other deities on one hand and Christian deities on the other.

The problem arises between polymorp "only." The former does not accept the word "only." It disagrees with that word. A believer in polymorphous monotheism cannot agree with the spirit of statements like: "God took only one form," "God appeared only once," "this particular form of God is the only redeemer." Rather, the substitute "also" instead of "only" is used. "This" form as well as "that" form.

Yadaayadaahi dharmasya glaanir bhavati bhaarata
Abyutthaanam adharmasya tadaatmaansham srjaamyaham[4]

Whenever there is a decline of virtue,
wherever there is a rise of evil,
for the protection of virtue
I send forth a particle of my Self

How many parts are in this atmaansham cannot be counted. This is where the practical approach of Hinduism to other religions is helpful. When I teach meditation to Christians, traditional Christian words like Jesus or Ave Maria or the Aramaic maranatha are used. When I teach Muslims, Allaho or one of the ninety-nine names of God that the Sufi pirs[5] may assign to their murids are used. When I give initiations in Buddhist countries—in Korea and Taiwan—Buddhist mantras are given. This is because the duty of a monk of the Swami Order is to strengthen a Christian's faith in Christ, a Muslim's faith in Allah, a Buddhist's faith in Buddha, and to help each adherent to realize the deep spirituality that is beyond religions.

It can be safely said that it is through polymorphous monotheism that we may rediscover the spirituality beyond religions. It becomes an umbrella for all paths.

The supporter of polymorphous monotheism always finds it easy to facilitate "conviviance" (used here as a neologism for "living together amicably") among those of varying religions. A wise elder in an African village continuing to give healing by the traditional methods has no objections to his devotees going to a mosque or a church.

Much is said about the current Hindu-Muslim conflict, but the "conviviance" the Hindus and Muslims have developed with each other, because the philosophy of polymorphous monotheism is still dominant in India, is not being reported. From the very precincts of the Delhi airport, one can see melas, religious fairs, going on not faraway. Walking down to the religious fair, I discovered it was being held around a dargah, the shrine of a Muslim holy man. On one side of the grave, the Muslim priest was reciting the Quran, and on the other side, the Hindu priest was performing a homa, a fire offering. Where else in the world would one find two religions performing two completely divergent liturgies, one in Sanskrit and one in Arabic, at the same shrine simultaneously. This is a daily occurrence in India, from long before the times when the word "secular" was introduced politically.

Even some strictly monotheistic paths may use many names for God derived from the traditions of polymorphous monotheism. For example, the Holy Book Guru Granth Sahib (Singh, 1989; Veda Bharati, 1998), a statement of One God par excellence, uses thirty-six different names for divinity including Brahman, Allah, and Khuda.[6] For a more detailed understanding of polymorphous monotheism, read God (Arya, 1979).

It is not reported how the peoples of 2,700 major ethnic groups and thousands of their offshoots, along with all the religions of the world, share one single country in a geographical area the size of Europe (excluding Russia), with much greater variety of languages and cultures than that of Europe itself.

It is safe to say that for many contemporary inter-religious problems in the world, the followers of polymorphous monotheistic paths have much experience of the past to offer and to suggest solutions to many contemporary problems of conflict. Such experience of the vast regions of the world is based on the core belief of the polymorphism of one Divinity. Religions and their scriptures have been interpreted and reinterpreted many times over. Quite often the faithful do not really adhere to the spirit of their original scripture but rather to a particular school in exegesis. It is safe to say that even the Abrahamic religions acknowledge many different manifestations of divinity. A close look at the Bible (Holy Bible, 1982) will show in how many forms God has made his appearances, echoing the roots of polymorphous monotheism in Judeo-Christianity. To cite a few, God appears to:

1. Abraham:
   a. As a voice in a dream/vision (Bible, Genesis 15:1)
   b. To Hagar as an Angel, whom Hagar later identifies as God (Genesis 6:10-13)
   c. In human form (the apparition at Mamre) (Genesis 18:1-5)
   d. In human form, to wrestle with Jacob (Genesis 32:23ff)
   e. As a command—Abraham is to leave his people and travel to the land of Canaan (Genesis 12:1-2)
   f. At Mamre, sits in the tent door—Abraham washes his feet and makes a food offering (Genesis 18.1ff)

2. Moses:
   a. The burning bush (Bible, Exodus 3:1-6)
   b. I Am That I Am (Exodus 3:13-15)
   c. Pillar of cloud and pillar of fire (Exodus 19:16-25)
   d. As fire and cloud (Exodus 24:16-18)
   e. Sees God's "back" but not his "face." (Exodus 33:18-23)
   f. Cloud (Exodus 40:34 ff)

3. Ezekiel:
   Vaguely like a human form, radiant amber light (Bible, Exodus 1:27-28)

The most outstanding example of the multiple manifestations of God is as Father, Son, and Holy Spirit, to say nothing of the veneration of Mother Mary or the Greek word for the Divine Mother, Panagina, meaning "doorway to the divine." As we have said elsewhere, if three can be one, why cannot three thousand be one. The very concept of the trinity in God supports polymorphous monotheism. No doubt similar references will be found in the scriptures held in esteem by other branches of the Abrahamic religions.

There is hope that this kind of improved understanding of various doctrines will reduce the level of confrontation among religions. Tolerance would not be the right word for such an all-embracing view of life and belief systems. "Tolerating" someone does not always mean fully accepting that another's religion is as great as one's own. Even in interfaith gatherings we do not often hear the followers of religions state: "Your religion is as great as mine." The followers of polymorphous monotheism, however, say: "Your religion for you is as good as my religion is for me. Do continue to worship your divinity the way you have been taught to worship by your prophets and priests, and please accept that the way we worship has been taught by our Incarnations and spiritual guides." This attitude would help solve many current problems of inter-religious conflict.

Ukrainian Jesus with Gesture of Grace
Photo by Bhagvat Prasa

Buddha Peace Mudra
Photo by Sujit Mishra

Mother Mary, St. Mary's Basilica
Church, Shivajinagar, Bangalore,
India
Photo by Mr. Gurudutt

This poster was presented to the Egyptian Delegation on the occasion of Pres Sadat's Peace Mission to Jerusalem Nov 1977. The various symbols represent various religions.

PEACE SIGN – Crayon on Paper /Shalini Persaud/ 09
The sign is made up of the flag signs for N and D – Nucelar
Disarmament.

Photo by Lalita Arya

Indo-Trinidadian girl playing a Hindi hymn on West Indian steel drums.

From left to right: Dott. Tanzi, VP Club of Budapest, Italy: Lucai K. Vigiani, yoga teacher; Swami Veda Bharati; Laura Linzi, translator; Dott. Marco Romoli, Pres. Tempio per la Pace (Temple of Peace;) Dott. Eros Cruccolini, Pres. City Council of Florence. At the Palazzo Vecchio,
Photo by Cristina Nobile

CHAPTER 4
Peace In Diversity[1]

The root of comfort and happiness is virtue.
The support of virtue is in economy and polity.
The root of economy and polity is right governance.
The root of right governance is channeling the energies of the senses
in a contemplative and meditative way.
The basis of relationships from which such a way emerges,
and in turn, supports the same, is control of ego in humility and discipline.
It is the respect to mentors and elders that leads one
to re-channel one's ego and inculcates discipline.
It is thus that one gains experiential knowledge.
It is knowledge that leads one to cultivate oneself as a person.
Cultivating oneself is synonymous with self-conquest for one
who has not conquered and learned to govern just one mind, his own,
how would he govern a whole empire?
Such a governance of oneself leads one, naturally and effortlessly,
to success in all of one's undertakings and desired goals
whether material or spiritual.[2]
CHANAKYA'S SUTRAS ON POLITY (SRIKANTAN, 2007)
(paraphrase and reinterpretation)

The philosophies of constitutional and international law need to be developed primarily on the basis of the fundamental precept that peace in the individual mind is the unit that, joined with similar minds, is the true source of collective, social, and political peace.

A pragmatic adjunct to this thought is that the cultural experience of only a certain segment of the human family is, at present, used to develop the prevailing philosophy and laws. The experiences of very large parts of humanity are simply not taken into account. It is partly because those who wield power are uncertain as to how to balance unity and diversity. They can find their way out of the dilemma by recognizing that:

> One seeks to become many.
> Many long to unite.
> Unity leads to diversity.
> Diversity balances its many parts and aspects,
> By seeking to maintain a unity.

In other words, such philosophies as that of the Bhagavad Gita and the Tao Te Ching (Feng & English, 1972) state (paraphrased):

> The opposites, whether concepts or entities,
> are not opposed to each other;
> They complement and complete each other.

Without recognizing their complementary natures, each side remains incomplete, feeling empty, seeking to fill itself through destructive paths of aggression, violence, and conquest. To illustrate, several decades back, a parliamentarian of Sri Lanka, discussing the role of the Simhala and Tamil languages in that country, is reported to have said "one language, two countries; two languages, one country." He meant that if diversity is permitted, the country will remain united, but attempts at uniformity will divide the country.

In the vast history of humanity, many conquerors have tried to unite the world by resorting to a fallacious interpretation of unity, and all have failed. However, history seems to have a will of its own, or to paraphrase Tolstoy (2011): the divine will uses human history to fulfill purposes of its own.

The leaders of a society may initiate a certain process with one intention, but the end result turns out to be quite different. The centripetal and centrifugal forces of unity and diversity work in tandem, playing with each other, balancing each other in the long run, even though, for a short while, human acts may appear to fulfill the purposes that the leaders had in mind. Consider these examples from recent history:

- The Peace Corps was established to bring the message of America to the people in far-away, primarily Third World, countries. The Corps volunteers went to the villages of Asia, Africa, and South America. They not only disseminated American knowledge but experienced the different value systems in diverse local societies. These they brought back to the United States, leading to fundamental changes in the thinking of corporate leaders as well as the general population.

- Originally the English language was spread throughout the colonies with the intent to anglicize them. Many texts were translated by the missionary enterprise, or by sympathizers of the same, for the express purpose of showing the world how worthless the texts and the traditions of the local people were. The result was that the world was inspired by these texts. With a more benevolent intent, Indian practitioners have used English to spread alternative therapies, meditation, and yoga to the Anglophone countries. Leading Western figures in both literature and philosophy have come to recognize the true value of these approaches and techniques.

- The Chinese invasion of Tibet drastically altered the civilization of that land, sending its guides and leaders into exile. Instead of being destroyed as the invaders intended, Tibetan knowledge has spread worldwide, a knowledge that would otherwise have remained locked in the mountain monasteries.

- Colonial education has had the unintended result of producing a vast number of people who might rightly be called "world citizens." Whereas people in imperial countries and their present-day successors remain confined to the use of their own language (e.g., English or French) and literature, the people of ex-colonial countries still speak and produce enormous amounts of literature in their own languages as well as in English or French. The learned in these societies, for example, read the texts of their own traditional medicine in the original language and interpret it into the language of the former imperial lands. They are at home with ancient and modern art forms, traditional vastu systems of architecture and modern ones. No one thinks of giving a Nobel Prize to a litterateur who writes in Hindi, Tamil, Thai, or Khmer unless the work is translated into a European language. The writers of these languages continue to enrich themselves with French, English, and so forth. While constituting a large percentage of Bill Gates' staff, they practice their own ancient philosophies, reading the Upanishads (Ekadasopanisadah, 1966; Hume, 1971), Kung-fu-tzu, and Lao Tze.

It is thus that the ex-imperial cultures, whose economies still dominate the world, work from a place of great disadvantage when it comes to the globalization of culture. Any endeavor at political, constitutional, legislative, executive, and judicial unity needs to recognize the fact of an existing world citizenship and take advantage of the knowledge, experience, and wisdom that these world citizens have gained.

We need to address certain questions in a number of areas in trying to develop theoretical models for unity through a world government and parliament, rather than an appearance of unity through conquest.

For the past several centuries, we have observed simultaneous movements toward unity and diversity. The creation of Italy and Germany from diverse sovereign states is an example of unity from within. The Federation of Five Nations, the Iroquois Confederacy, would be another example, even if such unification is triggered in response to the pressures being experienced from external forces. It is the people and their leaders, not extraneous sources, who generate such movements for unification.

Then there are examples of unity imposed through conquest, accompanied by major dislocations of the original ethnic populations. The indigenous peoples of countries like Canada, the United States, Mexico, or Brazil are united in calling themselves Canadian or American or whatever nationality they might be, but such a unity is an imposition that does not reflect the will of the original people.

Another example of artificially drawn boundaries is that of the present-day nation-states of Africa, whose fate was sealed in the Berlin treaty of 1885 that was signed among the European nations. The boundaries drawn by the European powers cut through the traditional and natural land borders, sowing the seeds of civil war for the day when the Europeans would make the appearance of leaving.

As is well known, the formation of and developments in Yugoslavia, from the fall of the Hapsburg Empire to the current decade, can be cited as another example (with a slight variation of the same theme). It appears that for the past century or two, the forces of history have exerted themselves simultaneously in the directions of diversification and unification. At the end of World War II, there were less than fifty independent and nominally independent nations. The number of de facto and de jure nations is now beyond two hundred. Along with such diversification of nations, the beginnings of the unification of Europe can be seen, though this is yet to be concluded. Within this historical force of unification, again, a drive for the preservation of numerous sovereignties continues to be a major force. Also, the fragmentation of former Yugoslavia shows the strong activity of centrifugal forces within the range of the European Union's centripetal forces.

The question arises: how is humanity to establish a balance between these centripetal and centrifugal forces, between unification and diversification? Those who wield the power to draw the models for the future unity of humankind are strongly tethered to certain world views that have been imprinted on them by the universally prevalent education system (to be discussed in Chapter 8 titled "Education and Parenting for Peace.)" Other educational systems that have, through training and enculturating, turned humanity into a veritable garden of flavors and fragrances from so many flowers for the past five millennia or more, remain virtually ignored. Since the history of democracy is traced primarily to Athens and other Hellenic city-states, the development of constitutions and international laws of war and peace are regarded as Eurocentric. In this, we are depriving ourselves of the benefits of learning from the experiences of a multi-centric human civilization.

• Why Athens alone?

• What were the forms of democratic elections in the Federation of the Vajji and Licchavi Republics (gana-tantras) in the areas where the Buddha preached in the Sixth Century B.C.?

- What were, and sometimes still are, the forms of common consultation among the chiefs and their peoples in traditional societies?

- What were the rules of consultations and negotiations among different nations in the Americas, and did they not have laws governing the conduct of peace and war?

- How were the various ethnic groups represented in the courts of the Kings of Indonesia and Southeast Asia for more than a thousand years?

This shows that the kind of compassionate thought leading to codes like the Geneva Convention were actually developed thousands of years before. Consider the Laws of Manu (Doniger, 1991) (ancient undated text attributed to Manu whom the Hindus regard as the first law-giver) with reference to conduct in war:

> One should not attack with secret weapons...
> Nor with barbed ones,
> Nor with poison-smeared ones,
> Nor with incendiary ones.
> Nor shall one attack him, he who has climbed down from his mount, Nor an impotent one,
> Nor one who is clasping his hands [seeking mercy],
> Nor one whose hair is in disarray [unable to care for himself],
> Nor one sitting down,
> Nor one who says "I am all yours,"
> Nor one asleep,
> Nor one who has lost his armor,
> Nor one who is naked,
> Nor a weaponless one,
> Nor a non-combatant,
> Nor one who is fighting with another,
> Nor a mere spectator,
> Nor one whose weapons are rendered ineffective,
> Nor one distraught,

Nor one very wounded,
Nor one scared,
Nor one taking to flight,
Remembering the righteous way (dharma) of the noble ones,
Let him ever act without guile, and on no account treacherously.[3]
LAWS OF MANU (7.90-93, 104)

The same message is heard in the Mahabharata (Narasimhan, 1965) as follows:

Yudhishthira asked:
When a warrior assails another,
how should he proceed?
How should one undertake the battle, tell me, Grandfather?

Bhishma said:[4]

One should not fight one who is not wearing his armor.
Only one should challenge him, "shoot, I do so too."
If the opponent comes girded, one should gird oneself too.
If he comes with an army, then one should challenge him with
an army.
If someone fights clandestinely, one may fight clandestinely.
If he fights by righteousness (dharma),
One should fight with righteousness.
One should not oppose a charioteer with a cavalry,
Only a charioteer should oppose a charioteer.
One should not produce calamity,
Nor attack one who is afraid or one who has already been conquered.
The arrow should not be poison-smeared or barbed,
For these are weapons of the ignoble.
One should fight to the point,
Not become angry at one who wishes to kill you.
Nor should one attack if there is a dissension between good
people.

So that any of them might suffer a disaster.
Do not kill someone who is physically weak,
Nor one who has no offspring.
One whose weapon is broken,
One who has panicked,
Whose bowstring is broken or whose mount or chariot is
crippled, should not be attacked.
[One wounded] should be treated and healed in one's own realm,
Or may be escorted to his own home[land].
[One treated in one's own realm] should be released when his
Wounds have healed;
This is the perennial law (dharma).
One should fight with righteousness (dharma);
So Svayambhuva Manu has taught.

MAHABHARATA, SHANTI-PARVAN, 95.6-14

Converted to modern terminology, do these rules not parallel the Geneva Convention, though established millenniums before Geneva existed?

In other words, in order for us to find philosophical ideals on which the constitutions of world unity may be built, it is not desirable to depend only on Aristotle, John Locke, or Voltaire. They represent the philosophical stream of only one part of the world. In the slogan of "liberty, equality, and fraternity," where do we find their common denominator, spirituality? This is not to deny the validity of the teachings of these philosophers who have accomplished so much for the Western world, but it is now necessary to become universal and to take the most pertinent and beneficial parts of the teachings of Manu, Yajnavalkya, Tiruvalluvar, Kung-fu-tzu, Lao-tzu, and others, as well as texts like the Mahabharata. These will help to develop models that arise from cultural psyches, and that are based on historical developments pertaining to the humanity of the non-Western world. Unfortunately, for now, the genius of these cultures in the fields of practical and constitutional theory and experience is all but ignored by lawmakers and wielders of power.

Here are a few illustrations and comparisons, with examples from the history of political culture in many parts of the world, that are commonly ignored:

- France, a country that is small compared to China, still couldn't abolish royalty without resorting to the guillotine; yet, Sun-yat-sen, an avid reader of French political philosophy, abolished royalty in China to establish democracy without resorting to a regicide.

- Would the United States have achieved independence without armed confrontation? Contrast this Euro-American experience with that of India. Is not the example of Gandhi's leadership in achieving independence a model to be pursued? How do we popularize this model among the various groups who indulge in violence while fighting for justice.

- Would it have been possible to establish unified nation-states in Europe without sending the erstwhile kings into lifelong exile? In contrast, India, a country the size of Europe, apart from the parts of India directly administered by the British, had 600 territories ruled by kings. Some were the size of Belgium, Holland, or France, while some were only the size of Monaco, Andorra, or Liechtenstein. Upon the independence of India, leaders of the new nation persuaded all of these kings to renounce their power in order to join the democratic republic—with the exception of the Nizam of Hyderabad and the Nawab of Junagarh, where there was some reluctance that was later abandoned. The few remaining privileges these erstwhile kings retained were also later abolished. Many members of these royal families are now great industrialists, ministers, cabinet members in federal and state governments, ambassadors, and in other reputable positions.[5] What strengths of the cultural and political traditions lead to such a smooth transition on the Indian subcontinent, and what can be learned from this and taken to other parts of the world?
- One of the reasons India, with an estimated 2,700 main ethnic entities and thousands of subgroups, has maintained cultural cohesion, if not always nation-state continuity, is because the king was never a lawmaker.[6] Throughout history, he was the final enforcer of the laws of each community upon their respective members. This principle was followed

even during the time the Muslims became a power. Many wiser Muslim Kings applied Hindu law to the Hindus; similarly, Hindu Kings applied Muslim law to the Muslims (for example, it would simply not occur to them to ban headscarves).

• Some elements of the present-day constitution of India follow the Western model of "unity through uniformity." Some of the present attitudes violate the traditional Indian principle of "unity and peace through freedom in diversity." It is for this reason that so many little civil wars are taking place in the border regions of India. The sooner India abandons some parts of the Western model, and in some areas reverts to the traditional one, the sooner she will ensure long-lasting unity without rebellion from various ethnic groups. The current voices for a common civil code are in violation of the traditions of India.

• In creating a motto for a global nation or even a world confederation, e pluribus unum, one out of many, would be a good start. We also need to look at the Indonesian motto in Sanskritized-Bahasa (old Javanese): bhinneka tunggal ika—different but one, or many in one.

This is a quotation from an Old Javanese poem, kakawin Sutasoma, written by Mpu Tantular during the reign of the Majapahit empire somewhere in the 14th century. Kakawin or Kawya are epic poems written in Indian meters. This poem is notable as it promotes tolerance between Hindus (Shaivites) and Buddhists.

This quotation comes from canto 139, stanza 5:

Rwâneka dhâtu winuwus Buddha Wiswa,
Bhinnêki rakwa ring apan kena parwanosen,
Mangka ng Jinatwa kalawan Siwatatwa tunggal,
Bhinnêka tunggal ika tan hana dharma mangrwa.

It is said that the well-known Buddha and Shiva are two different substances.

They are indeed different, yet how is it possible to recognize their
difference in a glance, since the truth of Jina (Buddha) and the
truth of Shiva are one.
They are indeed different, but they are of the same kind,
as there is no duality in Truth.

SANTOSO (1975)

- In the same vein, the formulations of successful world constitutions in
non-Western countries should also be examined. For example, Malaysia
recognizes two parallel systems of law. The Muslim Malays are
approximately 50 percent of the population and have chosen to live by
Muslim law; they prefer to be left alone to live by their own rules. The
other 50 percent are Hindu, Christian, Buddhist, and indigenous peoples
who are free to practice their own religions and customs with the common acceptance of civic law modeled after the British system. In a recent
check of the 19 public holidays in Malaysia, only four were Muslim; the
rest were Hindu, Buddhist, Christian, and indigenous. The Malays are
living in a Muslim state and the rest live in a secular, multicultural state,
on the same land, yet hari raya, the song celebrating the Muslim holy day,
can be heard in non-Muslim establishments and is played with equal gusto. Also, the government provides all necessary supports for tai pusam,
the major Hindu festival in which half a million people go in a procession
to worship at the sacred Batu caves.[7]

- The United States, often legally and emotionally insistent on one language, forces its Spanish-speaking populations to suffer many disad-
vantages. India, with four times the population, has the denomination written in fifteen languages on the one-hundred-rupee bill. Thank
the wisdom of those who framed the constitution that the slogan "unity
through uniformity" has not yet fully made a home in the Indian mind in
spite of the lapses mentioned above.

If it was not for their traditional wisdom, South Asia would be divided,
not only into the seven states of the Southeast Asia Regional Committee,
but would be divided into as many countries as there are in Europe. Orissa and Kerala are, for example, as different from each other as Sverige and

Magyar. Despite a European cultural unity, Sverige, Magyar, and Helvetia insist on maintaining sovereignty, but India's parallel cultural cohesion keeps Uttaranchal, Orissa, and Kerala in one single nation-state.

Why speak of a giant nation-state like India when even the city-state of Singapore, with a population of over four million (July, 2004 estimate) has four official languages: English, Malay, Chinese, and Tamil. One may choose to send a child to a school that teaches in any of the official languages. As one lands at the Singapore airport, some female immigration officers are wearing headscarves, others bindis (the red dot that Hindu women wear). The same is true of female police officers. The Kuala Lumpur airport is no different in this regard. One observes the same welcoming phenomenon, including an immigration officer wearing a Sikh turban at the London airport.

Here, if we have not given sufficient space to the countries of Africa, it is simply out of the ignorance perpetrated by the world educational systems. At this time, not enough is known of the contribution of African philosophies, even unwritten, informing the constitutions, national policies, and leaders of the people. One reads of the civil wars in the Congo, Rwanda, Burundi, or Nigeria, but no one tells the world how Benin, the land of an ancient civilization, with a population of over seven million and over 50 languages, lives in peace by following the principle of unity and peace through diversity. Is the validity of a culture dependent on its wealth?

Two examples, out of numerous others, of the greatness achieved through the guidance and inspiration of the African traditions are those of Nelson Mandela and Kofi Annan. Mahatma Gandhi is quite accurately cited as a source of Dr. Mandela's inspiration, but why his own very positive African heritage not recognized remains a puzzle. According to Richard Stengel, collaborative editor on Mandela's (1994) autobiography, *Long Walk to Freedom:*[8]

One of the things that he [Mandela] absorbed there [in his tribal environment] was this ability of the chief to listen to what everybody had to say. The chief didn't speak until everybody had had their say, and then he sort of weighed that. One of the things that was reflected in the negotiations, is that Mandela didn't weigh in with his opinion until everybody had spoken…in negotiations, in politics, he's enormously patient and part of that comes from his upbringing as a boy and seeing how the chief listened to what everyone had to say.

The concept of truth and reconciliation, as developed by Dr. Mandela and His Grace Archbishop Desmond Tutu, is mainly derived from the traditions of arbitration practiced by the civic and administrative leaders of the African village society. Nations would do well to study the attitudes and philosophy of the indigenous African traditions to help solve not only the problems of Africa but other areas of conflict around the world. Kofi Annan is not just a product of Macalester College and M.I.T., but his personality is strongly rooted in the wisdom of the African tradition:

Se eye ndzeye pa enum yi a, na eye barima.
Gather the five virtues, then you are a man.
FANTE PROVERB (E.G., CHRISTENSEN, 1958)

The five virtues he lists are:
a. enyimnyam: dignity
b. awerhreyemu: confidence
c. akokodur: courage
d. ehumboror: compassion
e. gyedzi:[9] faith

As we have seen above, greatness is not to be thought of as a monopoly of specific cultures. The models to be examined for forming a world confederation and, eventually, a global nation-state, must include the wisdom and experience of all lands and peoples, not only of those powers that have been dominant for the short period of the last two-and-a-half centuries. This goes to show that many of the neglected constitutions and policies of the less prosperous (like India) and the more prosperous (like Singapore), as well as the more populous (like India) and the less populous (like Singapore), can serve as models to be examined in framing a world constitution.

Returning to Asia, the Buddhist kingdom of Thailand is exemplary, being the only country in Asia that remained independent during the time of the colonial empire.[10] How did Thailand avoid the damage that other Asians suffered during the Japanese occupation? Why are such long-term diplomatic successes, with a strong background of personal and national philosophies practiced in these lands, not given as much prominence in the history of diplomacy as the records of success in European experience? The Buddhist spiritual guides have always played a major role. The king has to be trained in the ideals of renunciation as a young boy, since he must spend a number of months as a novice monk during his youth. Mentioning the Buddhist philosophy of Thailand brings us to the question of the relationship between church and state. In developing a universal model for a world with a rich diversity, the discussion should be expanded to include the role of philosophy and philosophers in the running of a state. For this we need to look at the dialogues of Socrates, as well as the philosophers in Asia, who have guided many kings.

The thinkers of Asia would not agree that philosophers should become kings. They would propose that the kings (statesmen and stateswomen in modern times) should be advised by the philosophers, and as they grow in wisdom, these kings should themselves become philosophers.

One example of the success of this model in the West is that of Marcus Aurelius, who shines as a man of wisdom apart from the long array of arrogant Roman conquerors. He could be cited as the exception that proves the rule.

In India, there is a long tradition of philosopher kings, or rajarshis such as Janaka, whose court in Vedic times was the gathering place of philosophers: Ashoka, who declared unilateral disarmament, disbanded all of his armies, and ruled over an empire the size of Europe through spiritual wisdom; King Bhoja, it is said, would allow no one to enter the capital city who could not create instant poetry; all the way down to the kings of the Chola and Pandya dynasties, and the royals of Travancore-Cochin, who were litterateurs, poets, playwrights, and authors of commentaries on philosophical texts.

There is a strong tradition in India, not equally observed in all areas and periods of history, where the counselor to the king lived the life of a renunciate, so that his advice would not be tainted by personal self-interest. The relationship here is not between church and state but between the precepts of philosophy and duties of the state.[11]

The success of such a philosophy in global statecraft will not be derived only from what is enshrined in constitutions and then drafted into legal codes. Its success will have to depend on conventions of personal ethics, where the training of leaders or statesmen and stateswomen would prepare them through education and personal ethics to act from within their conscience by the universal laws of applied spirituality (dharma).

This would require a much wider philosophy of education, one that incorporates the vast variety of educational systems that have prevailed, some of which are still struggling to maintain continuity in diverse human societies on all continents.

A common denominator in such a universally inspired education system, or a variety thereof, would be a spirituality that is separate from and beyond religion, that manifests in two important ways:

• as a common contemplative tradition practiced without violating any religious precepts, and

• as an applied spirituality in the form of ethical principles of renunciation and consequent nonviolence, compassion, equitable sharing, and so forth, to be practiced by those who lead political and commercial lives at whichever level.

To elucidate the same principles further,

1. Renunciation would mean:
    a. Renouncing ownership as a definition of sovereignty and replacing it with a trusteeship. The citizens, states, and nations would then be the sole trustees of earth, water, fire, air, space, and knowledge, sharing in the universal trusteeship of humanity.
    b. Nothing will be taken from Mother Nature without universal agreement that what we receive is not exploitative and

destructive but within the capacity of nature to regenerate. This is not the same as sustainable development that is a selfish commercial proposition, easily violated, and without any altruistic and intrinsic values based on the spirituality of nature and living beings.

   c. Since anger and violence arise from desire and fear,[12] educational systems will need to train citizens in the ideals of renunciation, universal love, and compassion, both through methods of contemplation and through exercises in personal ethics.[13]

2. The same principles of renunciation, compassion, and equitable sharing will guide global economic and commercial organizations to a code of ethics whereby:

   a. Organizations shall set rules for the workforce with a view to providing ample opportunity for developing both a positive family life and contemplative experience.

   b. Just as with Nature, so also with individual human beings or with groups and communities thereof—nothing shall be taken beyond their capacity. Such capacity is to be defined by whatever might be left over after providing the essentials of food, shelter, health care, education, and opportunities for developing a family and contemplative life on a worldwide scale.

3. The vastly diverse knowledge of humanity, as yet often unrecorded and uninterpreted, will be treated as the common heritage of humankind in the world confederacy or global nation-state. Such a state would not only provide all possible means for preservation and continuity for such knowledge but will also introduce lessons in the civic polity of the world. Without such a spiritual philosophy of contemplation, renunciation, compassion, and equitable sharing, it is not possible to create for humanity a full opportunity to benefit from the principles of "liberty, equality, and fraternity." As we have seen in the last centuries since the

French revolution, those three words are often used as props to justify their opposites in the relationship among various rungs of different societies. But this trend can be changed with a little wisdom from the philosophers.

4. Councils of philosophers will need to include not only official heads of well-known religious organizations and those renowned in ethical philosophy in a Socratic sense,[14] but equal place shall be given to the leaders in wisdom from the economically disadvantaged and less articulate indigenous parts of humanity (often patronized by being referred to with the euphemism "indigenous.") These councils of philosophers will guide the state. No laws shall be passed without the approval of the philosophers' council that, once again, will include representation of all schools of wisdom.

5. Through our understanding of spirituality beyond religion, we must not make the mistake of excluding those who follow a belief system that does not acknowledge a creator God. Several major religions (Buddhism and Jainism, for example) do not believe in a creator God but do believe in total altruism, self-sacrifice, and renunciation. Similarly, a number of schools of Indian philosophy do not discuss a creator God at all (for example, early Sankhya and Mimamsa), but inculcate the highest spiritual values. A scientist who believes in peace through altruism and renunciation, as given by the preceding definitions, is to be fully accorded the honor and privilege due to a philosopher.

This is by no means a prescription for a utopia. Even though a universal society based on these principles has not been established, many societies in different periods of history and geographical areas have successfully implemented at least some part of these principles in practical forms. An in-depth research project that is indifferent to the usual histories of wars and treaties will yield surprising values that we can learn. We can investigate why some succeeded where they did, why others failed where they did, and how to avoid the pitfalls of past failures, while repeating the historical successes on a universal scale. At the same time, we have the scientific means available to convert any of these principles into practical forms universally, while avoiding all that may violate the natural human urge for contemplation, compassion, and equitable sharing.

We suffer because we suppress these natural human urges. Let us cease to suppress them. Let us find ways to live by them. May we make human society a celebration of peace in unity through diversity.

CHAPTER 5
Two Diverse Religions in Dialogue

In addition to general statements about the unity of religions, we also need to explore the nature of dialogue between two or more specific religions. What follows, as a primary example, is such a dialogue between two culturally and historically diverse religions, namely Judaism and Hinduism, in order to see if a common ground can be found in doctrine, conduct, and experience between the two.

In such an engagement, the aim shall be to find those shared grounds where the world's most ancient faiths, Hinduism and the Jewish tradition, have met in the past (Vail, 2002), are meeting today, and may find further common interests in the future.

In this comparison, it is not necessary that these two religions agree on all points of doctrine and practices. Where they differ, may they continue to accept their differences. We do need, however, to emphasize those points where the two agree. Some areas to include and explore are:

1. The present dialogue is not a new effort in a historical vacuum. There is circumstantial and literary evidence of cultural as well as commercial exchanges between the two peoples going back several thousand years before the Christian era. Katz and Herzog (2007) give a very brief summary of references to India found in the Bible (Holy Bible, 1982), the Talmud (Verber, 1990), and the works of Jewish philosophers.

   Two of the Indian emperor Ashoka's (third century B.C.) rock inscriptions are bilingual—in Sanskrit and Aramaic, the latter being the lingua franca of then West Asia. This can be taken as circumstantial evidence of the connections between the people of West Asia and India at that time.

The story of King Solomon's wisdom about a dispute between two women, who each claimed to be the mother of the same child, is found in almost exactly the same form in the Jataka[1] tales of the Buddha in the Sixth Century B.C. Many other examples of this kind can be given.

There is thus a long history of relationships between the two religions.

We need to look at the amicable relationships that developed between the Hindus and the Jews in India. See Skolnik (2007), Jewish Virtual Library (2008), Katz (1994), Kunhikrishnan (2003), and Weil (2002).

These publications give a detailed history of the relationship of Jews with the Hindus including, for example, the grants made by Hindu kings for the construction of synagogues, and the adaptation of Hindu customs by the Jews where these did not conflict with the fundamentals of the Jewish faith.

One of the most beautiful examples of the sharing of Jewish and Hindu cultures is found in Johnson and Sakkariya's (2004) *Oh, Lovely Parrot! Jewish Women's Songs from Kerala*. The Indian Jews who have migrated to Israel can provide valuable counsel on the subject of the dialogue. The article by Katz and Herzog (2007) provides an excellent summary.

2. Hundreds of Israeli youths come to India nowadays to study yoga and meditation practices. There are also numerous yoga centers in Israel, not to mention the large number of Jews who attend yoga classes worldwide. The practitioners of yoga and meditation can give deep insights into how they reconcile their own faith with the greatest gift India has given to the world, namely, yoga and meditation.

3. The areas for this dialogue include the cultural and historical-political realms, as well as religious belief systems and spiritual practices.

Culturally speaking, here are some very select examples:

- Both cultures emphasize the closeness of the family.

- In both cultures, there is a special ceremony for boys to give them access to the Holy Scriptures, Bar Mitzvah in Judaism and Upanayana in Hinduism (Bar Mitzvah is one of the 613 mitzvot, rules of conduct, much like the Hindu smrtis.)

- Weddings in both cultures are held within a mandala-like enclosure with a similar canopy.

- The ritual form of veneration given to the holy book of the respective faith is often identical in both religions, such as placing the book on an altar-like space that has been consecrated.

- In both cultures, priests are married men, and no religious ceremony is complete without both spouses participating together.

- In both cultures, daily recitation of set prayers is a common practice.

4. Followers of both religions have a cultural flexibility whereby they have adopted the customs and practices of the countries of their respective diaspora, where these customs do not contradict their own traditions. That is why the Jews of India and Ethiopia are very different from those of Germany and Russia. The same classical acculturation applies to the Hindus of Nepal, Bali, or Manipur, as well as those of Guyana and Kenya in more recent centuries; both groups are different from each other and, yet, the same. This is seen even in their adaptations of personal names in their

host countries; German Jews have German names, Russian ones have Russian names, and the Jews of Ethiopia have names that are partially Amharic-sounding. It is also common for a Hindu named Sushil to, in Guyana, say that his name is Cecil. In other words, in both religions, there has been a desire to merge with their host communities without losing their respective interior identities. Followers of both religions thus present an example of flexibility in the preservation of identity.

- This principle of cultural flexibility practiced by followers of both religions has been seldom recognized by host communities worldwide.

5. Politically the followers of both religions have suffered persecution for many centuries at the hands of the fundamentalists of other religions, and have yet survived.

Both are non-proselytizing religions and do not seek converts. In the recent century or so, the more reformed streams in both religions have begun to accept a few converts on rare occasions.

6. A study of the passages and narratives in the Bible that are parallel to those in the Hindu-Buddhist scriptures needs to be made. For example, words for meditation occur 18 times in Genesis, Joshua, Isaiah, and the Psalms; of these, the 119th psalm is the most emphatic with the word meditation repeated seven times. The "Song of Songs," in its mystical interpretation, parallels the Hindu concept of the soul as the bride of God. There are hundreds of such parallels to be found in the Torah (Charing, 1993), the *Books of Wisdom* (Alter, 2011), Talmud, Mishna (Neusner, 1991), Midrash (Hammer, 1995), as well as the Zohar (Simon, 1984) and other such mystical works.

7. Numerous rivulets and streams of belief and spiritual practices are identical in spirit, if not in form, between mainstream Judaism

as well as Kabbalah (Franck, 1940), on the one hand, and Hindu traditions on the other. For example,

- the concept of Shekinah, the feminine force, that parallels the feminine shakti,[2] that, like the maya of Brahman, separated from the transcendental God, dwells as the spirit in the body of the universe and in living beings.

- the concept of the divine origin of speech.

- the mystical meanings and numbers associated with letters of the alphabet.

- the same letters associated with different parts of the body and psycho-spiritual personality.

- Ein Sof is the same concept as Brahman, Infinity, or Eternity. On this shared fundamental concept of Judaism and Hindu philosophy, numerous books can be written with parallel texts side by side.

- Ayin expresses shunya (neti.) This is another concept that many Jewish mystics who have experienced God share with the fundamental concept of "neti, neti" of the Upanishads (Ekadasopanisadah, 1966; Hume, 1971). Here again, volumes can be produced showing parallel texts. For example, Moses Maimonides, the celebrated author of Mishna, clearly favors the via negativa. Describing the doctrine held by Maimonides, the article "Jewish Thought and Philosophy" in the *Encyclopedia of Religion* (Dan, 2005) states: "The core of Maimonides' conception of God is a radical defense of the via negativa: the most accurate and appropriate way to speak of God is to say what he is not. Human language is essentially incapable of describing the nature of God." This echoes the Hindu texts such as Ashtavakra-Gita (Byrom, 1990) and numerous Upanishads.

- The ten Sefirot, the divine emanations from which the creation proceeds, is similar to the concept of prajapatis, the creators of the manasa-srshti, the mental creation in the Hindu conceptualization of the genesis of the universe.

• The same ten Sefirot as limbs in the body of God is comparable to the Hymn to the Cosmic Person in the Rig Veda (10.90.1) (Kashyap, 2003), as well as to numerous other subsequent hymns and statements throughout Hindu literature. See also, among other sources, Nelson (1998).

• "All creation as the body of God" is held in both religions, as in the mystical interpretations of the most important Jewish prayer called the Shemah.

• Practice of the vocal and mental recitation, as well as the contemplation, of the names of God.

• Like the ardha-matra (final silent half mora) of Om,[3] the name of God being unpronounceable.

• God tells Moses "I am that I am," "I am" being His name. This corresponds to the repeated Upanishadic statement soham-asmi, "I am that."

• Belief in a future Messiah who will redeem the world, and rejoin that which has been sundered, is exactly parallel to the very firm Hindu belief in the future avatara named Kalki.

• According to Flavius Josephus, the historian par excellence of the Jews, all three sects of the Jews, namely the Pharisees, Sadducees, and Essenes, believed in the incorruptibility of the soul (a doctrine also adopted by the Gnostics). This doctrine is fundamental to the Sankhya-yoga philosophy.

• The story of the great flood is repeated throughout the Hindu scriptures. The only difference is that in the Hindu tradition, there have been seven such floods so far, and seven have yet to come. The great one who creates the beings anew after each flood in Hinduism is known by the name Manuh, whereas in Judaism it is Nuh.

- In the Bible's Book of Josephus (Chapter 8), there are 56 statements about the Essenes. Of these 56 statements regarding their doctrine and conduct, all but 12 are identical to the rules followed by the holy beings of India, whether they be part of established spiritual communities, such as ashrams, or adopted by free wanderers.

- Of the 613 mitzvot (rules of Jewish conduct; plural of mitzvah), on cursory examination, 137 are identical in both religions; 107 had parallels (for example, memorizing the Torah or the Vedas (Macdonell, Muller, & Oldenberg, 2005), reading the "holy scriptures" according to one's faith). The other 369 were not relevant to comparison, arising out of a difference in cultures and doctrine.

- Even on questions such as reincarnation, not commonly pronounced as a Jewish doctrine, possibilities of compromise have been suggested. For example, see Werblowsky (1995).

- An area where Hindu and Jewish attitudes are identical is the anecdotes of the Hasidim (see Buber's [Buber & Marx, 1947] "Tales of the Hasidim" and texts such as Nahman of Bratislav [Band, 1978]), and the reverence for them. The stories of the Hindu "sants," their methods of teaching, guiding, and helping are identical in spirit to the stories of the Rebbes, Hasids, or Zadiks. Also the deep reverence accorded to both is identical.

- For meditation as a bridge between the two cultures, see Kaplan (1978, 1982, 1985).

- The hexagram, or Star of David, the symbol of Jewish identity, is an important symbol in both Hindu religion and meditation practices. In religion, it represents the union of upward ascending forces (fire as well as the masculine in the universe—shiva), and the downward descending ones (water as well as the feminine—shakti). This union of fire and water represents the union and balance of opposites in the universe, also seen that way in the mystic explanations in alchemy. It is interesting to note that in the Kabbalah, one of the many interpretations of the Star of David confirms the above, describing that, in the Zohar tradition, it represents the sixth Sefirot of the male (Zeir Anpin) united with the seventh Sefirot of the Female (Nekuva). In the Indian traditions of meditation, it is the line drawing of the spiritual force field in the heart center of consciousness on which the yogi may concentrate.

We are not here to discuss whether Kabbalah was revealed by Rabbi Simeon bar Yohai in the Second century, by Moses de Leon in Provence in the 13th century, or refined by Yitzhak Luria in the 16th Century; however, the parallels in the thoughts partially listed above are striking. See Katz (1994) for a further discussion on topics related to the Hindu-Jewish dialogue.

The above may be treated simply as notes to indicate the vast areas that call for more detailed research. There is no question that the two most ancient cultures have often shared common experiences, both in the mundane and the mystical realms, and it is now time for us to revive these ancient connections.

Similar common referents can be found between any two religions. For practical purposes of actually bringing people together in mutual understanding, scholastic exercises are not required, but, rather, a comprehension and deep realization among the common people that divinity has shown many faces to many of her children, and some of these faces that have manifested are identical. Religions are not identical, but not altogether so different as to lack common grounds on which mutual understanding may be built among the millions. It will be interesting to observe, for example, points of unity between Islam, on the one hand, and Hinduism or Buddhism on the other, on lines similar to the ones we have taken, for illustration only, with regard to Judaism and Hinduism. The same comparison can also be made with any two or more religions.

CHAPTER 6
Truth and Reconciliation

At interfaith gatherings, one is often tempted to perceive the followers of other faiths as an audience that may be tactfully and diplomatically preached to rather than a group with whom belief systems may be shared. We might even be tempted to use the message of tolerance and interfaith understanding to disguise our belief in our own uniqueness. Then we may go home and continue to tell our followers: all religions are great, but ours is still the greatest. In this process of religious arrogance, we might exhibit the age-old habit of:

1. Choosing the best and most inspiring passages from our own texts and the most creative and beautiful periods of our history, and

2. Comparing them with the worst passages and periods of history from the followers of an opposing religion.

In return, those to whom we are opposed use the same tool, citing the best examples from their own scripture and history, while attacking those of their opponents.

However, a true and sincere person seeking a lasting peace through religion will require that we draw upon some age-old practices known to all religions such as:

    a. confession
    b. apology
    c. repentance
    d. atonement

It could be suggested that:

1. The followers of each religion institute a series of seminars in which theologians and historians of the given religion present their research on:

    In what subtle or gross manner "we" perpetrated acts of injustice, exploitation, and violence toward the followers of other religions, especially when we were the victors and they were the vanquished.

    Let the leaders of the said religious communities make an open confession of these transgressions to the world at large and to the other religious communities that were the subject of such exploitation and violence.

2. This confession may even take place in a gathering of representatives of the two religions involved, followed by an apology in humility. In humility, we become truly great; in trying to prove ourselves great, we invite humiliation.

3. Acts of repentance and atonement may have the following forms:
    a. Giving recognition and honor to those whose conscience directed them to risk the wrath of their own communities by not participating in collectively hateful acts, and even helping members of the opposite communities in times of crisis.
    b. Setting aside a sacred day of silence and prayer on which the members of the two or more communities gather together and join in prayer and ceremony conducted by followers of the "other" faiths.
    c. Examining and confessing whatever acts of injustice or persecution may have been committed during the year.
    d. Renewal of a vow each year to protect the followers of other faiths and to enhance the opportunities for them to present their belief systems from the pulpit or in their education systems.
    e. Renew everyone's faith in freedom of religion and thought,

freedom from the fear of injustice and persecution.

f. Seeking God's forgiveness, on all occasions of prayer, for "whatever acts of injustice and violence we may have committed against the followers of other religions as passive or active participants," and to ask for "the strength, wisdom, and inner peace whereby we may prevent ourselves from doing so again."

g. If "our" religion is found to have destroyed others' places of worship, burned their books, or dishonored them in any way, then "we" contribute to the restoration of what can be restored or rebuilt in greater magnificence. The contribution may be in the form of funds or a labor of selfless love.[1]

h. Finding ways whereby the economically disadvantaged and less articulate religions, whose literature is often oral and mnemonic, have an equal opportunity to be represented where their voices may be heard, to advise in international forums such as the United Nations, UNESCO, and the International Court of Justice, on matters of ethics and philosophy, and that they be rendered economic assistance and the opportunity to interpret their language and idiom to make it accessible to all. It is known that Nelson Mandela derived much of his inspiration from within the African traditions, and Kofi Annan is also known to quote from his tradition to explain his decisions (see *Time*, 2000). Care should be taken that the importance of a religion is not based on its financial strength or the number of followers but on the true greatness of ideas and positive influence on humanity. The identity between ethnicity and religion should be considered invalid.

i. Scholars and theologians should examine the tools of exegesis whereby scriptural passages may be re-examined so as not to be interpreted as admonitions to destroy holy objects of other religions, of eternal condemnation, and others.

All the preceding recommendations will require a tremendous amount of faith in the universal compassion of God and the moral courage to make such a confession, to render apology, to undertake repentance internationally within the organizational structures of the religion, and to make atonement.

May we be granted this wisdom.

CHAPTER 7
Interfaith Unity in Meditative Silence

Blessing of Interior Peace

Without interior peace, the exterior environment of peace cannot be established. This Blessing is a collective experience of interior peace and silence to be guided for three to five minutes according to a universal contemplative system.

This meditation follows the one essential practice common to all contemplative systems such as Yoga, Vipassana, Zen, Ch'an, Tao, Sufi Dzikr, and Hesychasm in the Greek and Russian Orthodox tradition as taught in the Philokalia (Nicodemus, 1979) literature, and acknowledged in the Catholic faith as the "Third Method of Prayer" in the Spiritual Exercises of St. Ignatius of Loyola (Ganss, 1991).

This can also be a participatory demonstration of how all religions equally share a certain essence in the contemplative path that leads to interior peace, stillness, and silence.

The ultimate unity in God is to be found in contemplative and meditative silence. Let us share in this unifying silence together:

Please bring your awareness only to the space that the temple of
God, your body, is occupying;
Eyes closed lightly.
Both feet on the ground.
Rest your hands lightly on your thighs or on your knees.
Enter the silence within.
Choose a word or phrase from your own tradition.

113

Some suggestions are as follows:

1. Those who wish to follow the Himalayan tradition may use the sound-word "so" during the in-breath and "ham" during the out-breath, without a break in the cycles of "so-ham" with the breath.

2. The Sikhs may use Vaah-e-guru or Sat-naam.

3. Muslims may use the word Allah or any sacred phrase (such as La-Illah-illillah, or Allaho or Allahoo), or one of the 99 names of God.

4. Jews may use Ha-shem.

5. Christians may use one of these: Jesus or Yeshu, Hail Mary, Ave Maria, Maranatha (Aramaic), or Kyrie eleison (Greek).

6. Mazdayasnians (Zoroastrians, Parsees) may use any of these: ahura mazda, ahuu va-iryo, or esham vohu. But for total beginners of the Mazdayasnian tradition, the best recommendation is to use the phrase vohu-mano.

7. The Jains may use Om, Om hreem, or Hreem arham.

8. Those who prefer total nirguna, that is, transcendental, trans-qualitative divinity may use only Om.

9. The Buddhists may use the word Buddho to start with.

10. The Theravadin Buddhists may choose to use no word whatsoever; they may only practice mindfulness of breathing.

11. If you do not believe in a form of divinity or spiritual incarnation and so forth, exhaling, think Oooonnne (One) inhaling, think Twwwoooo (Two) without a break in this count with the breath.

Now with the eyes closed, relax your forehead.
Feel the flow and the touch of the divine gift called the breath.
Feel the flow and the touch of the breath in the nostrils.
Breathe gently, slowly, smoothly.
When you come to the end of a breath, let there be no pause.
Immediately begin to feel the next breath.
While feeling the flow and the touch of the breath in the nostrils,
think the sacred name or phrase you have chosen.
Not in the mouth or on the tongue. Only in the mind.
Breathing out, think that name, and without a break, breathing in,
think that name.
No break between the breaths.
No break in the thought of the divine name along with the breath flow.
All conflicts of the mind settle down and merge into the flow
of a single stream.
For a moment, cease all "method," all effort.
Let the mind become a chamber of silence.
Listen only to this silence for as long as you wish.
Again, continue to feel the breath with the divine name as a thought.
Observe how the mind, Name, and the breath are flowing together
as a single stream, the entire mind becoming an even flowing stream.
Maintaining the flow of this stream, gently open your eyes.
Let the flow of silence and peace continue.
Thus may the people of all faiths pray together in silence.
Only a mind at peace will generate peace among religions, ethnicities,
and the various peoples.
Resolve to be the source of that peace.
Maintain the flow of this awareness.
I pay homage to those Masters of the past thousands of years who
have, in the same manner as here, gathered many times in history
to bring and string together the peoples of manifold doctrines and
rituals into a single stream of peace and silence.
I pay homage to you all, the fellow waves of divine light.

CHAPTER 8
Education and Parenting for Peace

The basic ideas presented in this work address contemporary concerns within the context of what Aldous Huxley (1970) called the "perennial philosophy," an attempt to formulate concepts that are not meant to provide solutions to problems, are not for preventing wars, nor for pre-empting the next act of terrorism, but are meant to help search for a way of life for human beings, a modus vivendi, in which these problems cease to arise because of an internal evolution in the spirit of the homo comtemplatiens.

These presentations and proposals arise from the lineage of the Himalayan Yogis and all other such contemplative traditions worldwide that are agreed on their perennial values.

One of the purposes of these publications is to evoke a response from those endowed with the power and mundane means to help support the concepts presented through detailed and methodically organized research, and to develop practical ways to institute the ideas presented so as to benefit the global society.

The thoughts offered here are brief notes, almost in the category of mnemonic devices. Each paragraph waits to be developed in full, requiring a complete chapter of its own—a field of opportunity for those who seek "problems" to solve in their doctoral theses. Studying the variety of educational systems and incorporating their strengths into mainstream education will on its own enhance peace to a great extent.

Some of the suggestions made here maybe too "spiritual" for some minds, but so were systems like Ayurveda and meditation thought to be "strange" just a few decades ago. Now they have found a respectable place in mainstream Western society. Slowly and steadily, the steps for applying these thoughts can be developed, starting with the most easily acceptable. It is hoped that the leaders of the prominent interfaith organizations such as the World Council of Religious Leaders (an off-shoot of the Millennium World Peace Summit, 2000), World Parliament of Religions, and such others will formulate proposals based on these concepts. The proposals may then be presented to and accepted by the United Nations, UNESCO, and others that guide the direction of humanity's future.

May the Beneficent One grant the bene to all living beings.

Mind: The Locus of War and Peace

It is well recognized in the United Nations and elsewhere that it is in the minds of human beings that wars originate and only in minds that they can be prevented.

At the time the United Nations was founded, humanity was just emerging from World War II. Naturally prevention of war and not defining terms such as "peace" or "mind" was the primary concern for leaders at that time. They seem to have missed out on emphasizing that preventing war is not synonymous with establishing peace.

The philosophical aspect of this and other such concerns has not been developed any further. Nations and ethnic and religious groups and their leaders have yet to arrive at a clear understanding of and agreement about the various aspects of educating minds for peace. Here we attempt to advance some formulae that are centered on defining the terms: peace, mind, and education.

Definitions

Peace is not to be defined merely as an absence of war, or a period between two wars. So what exactly is peace?

Peace, like love, is experiential. We know experientially when we are in love. So do we know when we are at peace. Both love and peace are indefinable but, for the sake of convenience, let us propose that:

Peace is a state of consciousness: mind that is free of internal conflict(s) within an individual, as well as collectively, and consequently, among groups of individuals known as nations, religions, ethnic units, and other such terms.

What is Mind?

Mind is a force within individuals, not necessarily the sum total of brain activity, but a holistic power more than the sum total of all its constituents that serves as an instrument of sentience and conscious-ness to accomplish, through the intellectual and physical faculties, whatever consciousness may choose through its freedom of will.[1]

The mind includes all intuitive, rational, emotional, and neurological functions.

The mind can be trained to perceive, comprehend, and interpret any internal or external event, experience, or memory in diverse ways, the choice of which, for the individual, is often determined by the social groups that hold common belief systems. These groups apply various conventions and methods for imprinting their choice upon the individual mind. This imprinting is commonly known by such terms as training, acculturation, and education. Parenting is a primary part of such imprinting, with all other such systems being subsidiary.

A free mind is a peaceful mind that:

1. does not respond to mental imprinting that may lead to internal and, consequently, external conflicts;

2. remains free of conflicts, in a state of harmony that includes apparently conflicting aspects of truth and reality as contributing and complementary parts of a holistic system.

Unfortunately, most minds and their mutual associations are not free, but subject to such socially induced imprinting as appears to benefit the particular social, ethnic, religious, or national grouping. A mind is free to the extent to which it does not act or react merely from the force of such conditioning.

Education for peace in planet-wide system(s) would consist of:

1. imprinting minds so that they hold a holistic view of all human experiences (memory, histories, traditions), thoughts, and belief systems as constituents of a single whole, and

2. facilitating all imprinting that leads to freedom from conflict within an individual mind and, consequently, among social, ethnic, religious, national, or other groupings.

Peace: A Basic Urge

Any system of education needs to be developed, not merely on the basis of an assumption or hypothesis, but on these observed and confirmed facts:

1. An urge toward love and peace is intrinsically intuitive as well as instinctive for all sentient and conscious beings, many seeking to be One.

2. However much suppressed or distorted, this urge will always manifest its force in one form or another.

3. Often lying concealed as a potential, it may be developed and made fully operative through the presentation of positive and harmonious stimuli and holistic conditioning called education for peace.

It must be recognized that even in a cataclysmic conflict between two groups, it is the force of the same love that provides bonding within each group, even if against another. It is only that this force is being misdirected externally.

Here is an attempt to understand the sources of conflict:

1. All conflict begins within an individual mind when we each harbor mutually exclusive and conflicting ideas about external stimuli such as objects and events presented to us. Unable to resolve the conflict between two ideas, they are pitted against one another, and the mind continues in this manner, unable to view these ideas as complementary parts of a whole. For example, the opposites of day and night forming the complete planetary time cycles and systems.

2. After making our choice of personal attitudes, actions, reactions and memories, there is a preference to identify with some traits

and reject others. This produces a conflict of identities among different parts of our own being.

We project onto others what is "bad" by our definition (based on our past imprints). This we reject within ourselves but use it to identify the "other." With the projection and extension of our own "good" onto others, we identify and form alliances against the "bad other." This diversity, if not directed with and toward the beauty of love and the harmony called peace, becomes an antagonism, a condemnation of and challenge to the other. Thus it is that individual neuroses become acts of aggression, and, when socialized, become acts of aggression, terror, and war, leading us to a helpless "suicide pact" with the "other."

War and milder forms of antagonism are experiences and acts of collective neuroses generated because of the individual neurosis of leaders. Social neuroses are mutually supportive, feeding upon each other as the human family (or partial kinship structures thereof) becomes dysfunctional.

Whatever we do against our basic intuitive and instinctive urge toward harmony, beauty, love, and peace produces painful conflicts in our individual or collective mind(s). We continuously work to alleviate and eliminate the pain that is caused by ignorance as the Buddhist and Sankhya-yoga philosophies repeatedly emphasize.

The prime means to end the dysfunctional dynamics of the human family is to introduce a change in all minds through an education that instills a sense of peace, so that the basic urge for love and peace may find its fullest expression and satisfaction.

Sources for a Plan

A plan for education could be formed by:

1. Reading the writings of spiritual philosophers from all cultures who have given guidelines on education and training for a peaceful human mind.

2. Looking into the ancient histories of all continents to find examples of the ways that conflicts have often been resolved,

and developing ways to implement these lessons for solutions of contemporary problems.

3. Studying the internally accomplished psycho-spiritual developments of leaders in recent history who have succeeded in bringing about nonviolent change in situations that otherwise might have led to bloodshed. Studies should be made of the lives of leaders like William Penn (and other Quaker leaders), Gandhi, Martin Luther King, Lech Walesa, Mrs. Corazon Aquino, Vaclav Havel, Nelson Mandela, Bishop Tutu, Gorbachev, and numerous others. We need to look into:

   a. internal methods they employed for arriving at their personality, character, and the consequent public methodology,
   b. the advice of the surviving leaders,
   c. whatever can be found that has been written by or about the internal psycho-spiritual developments of the departed leaders so as to know how to include these methods in modern education systems.

4. Researching contemporary studies in social psychology that:
   a. indicate the mutuality between personal psychological conditions and social structures,
   b. draw some common conclusions from the same that will point to a new direction in education,

5. Interpreting world history as primarily the history of peace, even among the dominant civilizations, for example:
   a. How is it possible that the powerful civilizations of India and China, sharing areas of interaction at the borders that are, perhaps, 7,000 kilometers long, never had a war for 5,000 years until the aberration of 1962 (when the values of Chinese civilization were overwhelmed by the Marxist-Leninist-Maoist version of Western ideology)
   b. How did it happen that Kublai Khan, grandson of Changis

Khan, settling in Khanbalig (now Beijing), took instructions in the art of personal and social peace from Buddhist monks and Taoist sages?

    c. What wisdom guided, and what strategy was used, by Thailand (Siam) for it to remain the only country in Asia to be free of European colonial subjugation?[2]

    d. How did 600 kingdoms and principalities in the Indian subcontinent, some as large as France or Belgium, and others the size of Monaco or Liechtenstein, surrender their privileges without a bloody revolution and joined the Indian democracy in 1947?[3]

6. Observing the educational systems of countries:
   a. with plural societies where, together with total freedom of religion, a prohibition on criticizing any religion is strictly enforced (e.g., Singapore and Surinam);
   b. whose sovereignty is maintained without keeping an army, as in Costa Rica.

7. Creating the framework of a theory derived from peacemaking processes used in the empires of pre-Pizarro South America, or from the practices among ethnic entities of pre-Amerigo North America or pre-colonial Africa, and other such areas of the world whose history is at present dismissed merely as that of tribal warfare.

8. Studying different kinds of education systems that have developed among civilizations and cultures, extinct or contemporary; studying the role played by philosopher-kings in the dominant civilizations, be it Akhenaton, Ashoka, Marcus Aurelius, Harun al-Rashid, Akbar, or the Kings of Travancore-Cochin. Studying the ways these kings used to educate their citizens towards peaceful thinking and co-existence.

9. Observing the workings of education through:
   a. parents, and

b. wise men and women in religious and ethnic groups, such as the Jainas, Bishnois, and many others whose followers and members do not traditionally participate in wars and conflicts.

10. Establishing a World Council of Ethics and Peace under the aegis of the United Nations, UNESCO, the World Council of Religious Leaders, and leading interfaith organizations composed of:
    a. representatives of all religions and belief systems who believe in education for peace;
    b. all worldwide leaders of nonviolent change;
    c. Nobel Laureates who have received the Peace Prize;
    d. academia in the field of Peace Studies;
    e. philosophers, poets, and artists who have significantly advanced the idea of peace.

11. Inviting the representatives of organizations looking to establish peace, such as the Carter Center, the Club of Budapest, and all departments of Peace Studies in academic institutions, preferably through UNESCO and the United Nations' university campuses to:
    a. coordinate the results of the studies suggested, and
    b. formulate an all-inclusive, non-culture-specific:
        i. theory of education for peace,
        ii. worldwide plan for a system of education for peace, with practical steps for establishing such a system, with purpose and objectives to:
    a. help the plans for this education to be successful in all nations, through all systems of education;
    b. advise nations and their leaders on establishing and maintaining a peaceful world order;
    c. serve as arbitration counselors, mediators, and facilitators in situations of continuing or impending conflicts among any entities, whether existing de jure or de facto, without prejudice to the principle of sovereignty of any party in a dispute;

d. continue to develop, define, clarify, and advance in the world's consciousness, a philosophy of and methodology for peace and nonviolent progress;

e. advise all organs of the United Nations, as well as states and political entities, on the questions of morality and ethics relating to sovereignty, constitutions, human rights, and relationships, equitable distribution of wealth and opportunity, relationships among religions and ethnic entities, the environment, and so on;

f. achieve these results through a multi-lateral organization, the charter of which may be drafted and proposed by a group dedicated to these same ideals, and passed in the first assembly of a World Council of Ethics and Peace, as well as already established bodies within the United Nations.

Components of Education

In all systems of education, there are three components, each emphasized and developed to varying degrees in different systems:

1. Personality Development
   a. Helping the trainee develop a personal philosophy of and goal for life.
   b. Training for positive and harmonious emotions.

2. Gaining Knowledge
   Giving/receiving information in the areas of sciences and humanities, although the divide between the sciences and humanities is an artificial one, as science; up to the beginning of the 19th century, was classed under "philosophy."

3. Intuition and Inspiration
   In this intuitive-contemplative component are taught the methods for:
   a. mindfulness,
   b. concentration through relaxation,

c. enhancing the capacities of the mind,[4]
d. bringing all mental states under one's command:[5]
   i. bringing the mind into intuitive-contemplative states,
   ii. discovering for oneself that harmony and serenity, love and
      peace, are the innate natural conditions of the mind, and
   iii. learning to serve the world through such a natural state.

Unfortunately, the teaching of the last component is now rare, and the
first one is often placed on the back burner. Conflict resolution is often
taught as something to be obtained through self-assertion, encounter, and
confrontation rather than selflessness, humility, confession, apology, and
love in a peaceful mind. We often fail to realize the connection between
a twelve-year old child going on a shooting spree in school and a dictator
or president being responsible for the killing of innocent women and children in war.

This was not always the state of education.

Systems of Education

As stated, we take for granted whatever is imprinted upon our minds
by those who seek to limit the scope of our personal culture. So it has been
imprinted on our minds that education is what is imparted through books,
printed or electronic, and through audio visual mechanisms, in schools
and colleges built worldwide on a contemporary "Western" model.

Someone who sits by a village bonfire and recites an epic by heart,
a masterful work of literature by any standard of literary criticism, is
dubbed an illiterate if he or she cannot read the written word.

One is considered to be "educated" if he or she has read Shakespeare in
England, but not if one has read only a Thai masterpiece in Thailand. The
Thai Ramakien (Cadet, 1971) is somehow not equal to Milton's *Paradise
Lost* (Pullman, 2005), nor is *Lorikayan* (Singh, 1970)[6] or *Padmavat* (Malik
& Mataprasada, 1963; Shirreff, 1944)[7] equal to *The Iliad* (Mueller, 1984).
The history of political philosophy is taught as beginning with Aristotle in
Greece; the massive ancient works of India and China do not count.

There may be many "myths" of creation, for example:
"He divided Himself in twain."

By one half did He become woman,
by the other half did He become man,"

as in the philosophies of genesis in India, but the "real" human beings are thought to have been begotten only of Adam and Eve.

The widely held prejudice and disinformation that contemporary school systems advocate to be the only valid form of education, through which education for peace can be advanced, should be dispelled. The following is a partial and brief survey of a variety of educational systems that have existed historically, and some of which still struggle and survive.

1. The present-day Western school/college/university system does not represent a continuity of the ancient Western culture as was taught and practiced in:

2. The Greek tradition of philosophy, starting from Pythagoras (or perhaps Orpheus), going on through Socrates, Plato, Aristotle, and the Academy of Philosophy in Athens. Its philosophy of education could be applied in a modified form to add "spirit" to modern education and the system of Sparta from which are derived words like "gymnasium" and "gymnastics."

3. The ancient Chinese system of the "man-da-ren," anglicized to Mandarin, was the oldest system, not only of civil service examinations but of developing a Taoist-Buddhist philosophy of life and the personal and social ethics taught by lawgivers like "Kung-Fu-Tzu" (anglicized to Confucius). Its "Confucian" value system is responsible for the success of many East and Southeast Asian economies of today. Its study is much needed as an integral part of modern education systems for the applications of its relevant parts to contemporary political, economic, business, and family life.

4. The traditions of spiritual and philosophical training of children in lineages that have continued for millennia, such as the training of:

a. The Brahmin child, among the remaining few thousand families that still follow the classical systems,
b. the children of the Levites, the most philosophical of the twelve tribes of Israel,
c. all castes of India to give at least one child to an Udasi or dash-nami[9] monastic system, or to a Jain system, a family of Sikhs to offer one child for a life of self-sacrifice and service, giving a Jewish child after Bar Mitzvah, and a Mazdayasnian (Zarathustrian) child after the Navjot (there are other examples). Similar traditions exist in Buddhist countries, and were practiced in medieval Christianity.

5. The Madarsa and Maktab[10] systems of the Islamic world that have been much in the news of late as an anti-scientific seeding ground for terrorism. We forget that it is also the system that:
   a. produced philosophers like Ibn-cena (incorrectly spelled as Avicenna), whose work inspired the founding of the first medical colleges in post-Renaissance Italy;
   b. preserved Greek philosophy and medical systems after the burning of the library of Alexandria and the Christian Church/emperor(s) closing of the Athenian Academy of Philosophy. The works of Plato and Aristotle in their Arabic versions are still studied and debated among the most erudite in the Islamic academies in the pan-Islamic, including Iranian, systems.[11] The Greco-Arabic medical system known as Yunani (Ionian in the Greek form) is the traditional medical system (parallel to Ayurveda in India) taught in medical colleges of the Islamic world, from Malaysia and Indonesia to Morocco and Algeria;
   c. produced astronomers like Ulug Beg, whose methods of constructing an astronomical observatory were modified by the Indian Astronomer Maharaja Jaysingh, who created his own observatories in the 17th century;
   d. translated the vast array of Sanskrit philosophical texts, as well as such texts as Sushruta (Sushruta & Sharma, 1999),

the most ancient ayurvedic classic on surgery;

e. translated from Sanskrit and popularized Hindu mathematical systems such as zero (Buddhist shunya, Vedic kham), decimal (Sanskrit dashama-lava, a tenth part), algorithm (the word absorbed into Latin from the famous Arab mathematician Al Khwarizmi's translation of the Sanskrit texts), and other examples;

f. developed the beautiful traditions of exquisite Arabic calligraphy, illustrated manuscripts, and the impressive achievements of secular and religious architecture.

The above list is only an illustrative one. The right approach to solving the current problems arising from misinterpretations and misuses of these systems is not to close them down. In many countries with high levels of illiteracy, these systems alone provide a semblance of rudimentary literacy. The leaders of the systems need to be persuaded to study the history of the great scientific, philosophical, and literary accomplishments of their predecessors in order to have these institutions again serve as centers of free inquiry and advanced learning.

Just as they "then" assimilated the scientific aspects of the teachings of the Greeks and Hindus, they may "now" do the same with occidental systems of knowledge. They need not feel threatened by the loose moorings in their own theology, looking at how the Jesuits successfully advanced both scientific knowledge and traditional Christianity.

6. The training in arts and crafts that are passed on from parent to child, neither of whom may be able to read or write. The tradition of these hereditary craftspersons has produced exquisite works of art with the most rudimentary tools. These far surpass the beauty and execution of anything that graduates of modern trade schools can create using all the modern machine tools. The range of products in innumerable cultures cannot be listed, nor has there ever been a survey of these traditions of education. Some of this is passed on in comfortable surroundings such as those provided in Japan for the masters who have been declared National Treasures.

Then there is a vast majority in villages and towns, worldwide, who are struggling just to survive. The passing on of such traditional crafts requires total immersion on the part of the apprentice from very early and formative years. These traditions of rigorous discipline and concentration of mind in perfecting the relevant skills are threatened by:

a. the market economy, in which machine-made products win the competition through massive publicity as well as political and other stratagems of the powerful;

b. artists and craftspeople lacking basic resources so the younger generation is drawn to more lucrative vocations;

c. The fact that those who have mastered such skills have no equivalent of a trade school certificate and no place in the modern job market, and;

d. The reality that these traditions of education are further threatened by the proponents of child labor laws, as these proponents do not always discriminate between training the child as an apprentice, and working the child in a system of ruthlessly exploited child labor. The latter practice should be banished, the former protected, supported, facilitated, and enhanced.

This type of training is not imparted only to children, but there are parallel traditions for adults. One example among many is the apprenticeship of a zimmerman (carpenter) in Germany.

In all such traditions of education, the mastery of a skill is not the only goal. The mentor and trainer observe the psychology and character of the novice and train him or her for a balanced view of life. It is from this strength of the system that many lessons in our quest for education for peace are derived.

What has been said about forms of knowledge and education equally applies to numerous sciences, such as metallurgy and astronomy. The mystery of many metallurgic objects produced by traditional cultures is yet to be unravelled. The Polynesians sailed the Pacific guided by their knowledge of, it is said, up to six thousand stars. How was such knowledge passed on?

Again, it is noteworthy that all traditional knowledge is transmitted only to those who qualify, not merely by their ability to learn but, importantly, by their diligently cultivated inclination to share the benefits of knowledge unselfishly.

7. Besides arts and crafts, the many other areas of knowledge passed on outside the current school systems, such as the Bhats (Bards) of India and the Gerots[12] of West Africa, whose epic songs contain genealogies and histories of entire kingdoms. Their mnemonic devices are worth studying to help the modern-day student. Much needs to be incorporated into the modern system from their attitudes of life whereby they carry on the traditions in spite of the fact that royal patronage has been withdrawn in most cases. Similarly, we may learn from the methods of training their successors who are, again, tested for attitudes, virtue, and discipline.

Not all such traditions are treated equally today. The surviving portions of the Sumerian-chaldean epic *Gilgamesh* (Sandars, 1972) are available in many editions and translations, but these publications take no note of the folk singers of West Central Asia, who still sing the narratives that might be the modifications of the ancient Gilgamesh. What they have passed on for all these millennia, educating generations upon generations at great sacrifice, may really help complete our knowledge of the text. On the other hand, the case of a piece of Western literature is different. The national epic of Finland, Kalevala, was reconstructed by drawing together many sections and versions from the "folk" who had been educating many generations in this treasure of humanity.

The keepers of such rich repertoires are not all men. Thousands of "illiterate" women worldwide have been preserving and handing down numerous genres of literatures, histories, and songs that are liturgies of elaborate life-enriching sacraments and rituals.[13] There are, similiarly, a vast number of drama and dance forms, the education for which, orally transmitted and required tremendous discipline and development of personal character. Some governments have employed these "folk" singers to carry contemporary messages of reform such as literacy and health. The modern messages are composed in the ancient style to draw the attention of the millions who still respond to this form of richness. Those making a diligent effort for peace and mutual understanding among religious and ethnic groups have the option to use this worldwide medium for a purpose of high significance.

8. In the martial arts of the East, in Japan, Korea, and China, where the pedagogic methods used are not known in the popular Western school system. It is the student's character and temperament that count greatly in determining whether he or she is qualified to be given certain levels of knowledge. Total inner stillness, in a relaxed and calm mind, while the body moves swiftly, marks the candidate's success and, there is a vow never to use undue force that may hurt or harm beyond the necessity of absolute self-defense.[14] In this context, studying the teaching and training methods used in the martial arts of India such as Kalari,[15] Manipuri,[16] and the akhada[17] system would prove useful.

9. The equivalent of the M.B.A. in traditional trading societies, be they European, Jewish, Arab, Chinese, or Indian. In India, the history of international trade goes back 5,000 years to the port of Lothal on the western coast. It is known that, until the beginning of the 18th century just before European colonization began, 24.5percent of the world's production of goods was in India. Twenty-five per cent of the world's silver is in India, a country that has no silver mines. The world's largest stock of gold, including gold in the form of jewelery, is in India, and 20percent of all decorative gold of the world is in the saris that Indian women wear. All this wealth of India has been made possible with the entrepreneurship of the traders trained in traditional methods.

These traditional trading systems continue today alongside

modern commerce. The families of Sindh, Gujarat, Marwar, and Chettinad still maintain the tradition of training managers from their youth within the trading and banking family disciplines. Yet only a few anthropologists (not business management teachers) have studied their methods. For example:

a. Trade in silver and gold, worth millions of dollars, is still carried out in India without a single written word or contract of any kind. Whether in Surat or Tel Aviv or Antwerp, the Jewish and Indian traders carry out all of their diamond trading without any written exchange or invoices.

b. Some traders in many different countries have earned notoriety in evading income tax by maintaining a double set of books. However, the same traditional traders throughout the ancient markets of India maintain meticulous records for their daan-khaataa, the books for tithing, or giving 10% of their income from which temples, village wells, reservoirs, pilgrims' hospices, and other projects were built and maintained. It is from such resources that all the ashrams and thousands of educational, medical, and charitable institutions are still supported. There is never a question of evading this socio-religious duty.

Systems of education run by temples and monasteries throughout history have been the most neglected resources in formulating current educational systems. These systems include:

a. Himalayan cave monasteries, where the precepts of yoga, meditation, and related philosophies and texts are taught.
b. Schools, known as patha-shalas, attached to almost every village temple in India. These schools have provided both religious and secular education, such as liturgy to the would-be priests, accounting to the would-be traders, and so forth.
c. Buddhist school systems of Tibet, Mongolia, and other

countries that thrived until the Communist takeover. Similar systems in the Buddhist republics of the erstwhile Russian empire, and the contemporary school system of Thailand with its schools attached to temples and guided by monks.

d. Ashrams of the Swami and Jain orders of monks in India, dating back to 2,000 B.C., continuing to provide profound training in philosophy.

e. Coptic, Catholic, Greek and Russian Orthodox, and other Christian monasteries, some of which did not only maintain a religious life but preserved and taught classical languages; the art of calligraphy and illuminated manuscript; healing sciences including herbal lore and wine-making; thespian arts needed to stage passion plays; rudimentary meteorology, astronomy, mathematics; and teachings in other areas as well.

10. Schools of various medical systems of the world are being almost totally ignored. At least eight systems of medicine are taught and practiced in India alone, all equally recognized by the government:

a. modern medical colleges based on the Western medical model
b. ayurveda
c. naturopathy
d. homeopathy
e. siddha medicine of the Tamil tradition
f. tib (Greco-Arabic), also known as Yunani
g. Tibetan
h. Yoga

Each of these operates its own colleges and employs the traditional methods of discovery, continuity in education, and assimilation of modern methodologies of diagnosis, treatment, and research. More than 90% of the population of approximately 1.5 billion in the South Asian Association for Regional Cooperation (SAARC) countries of India, Pakistan, Nepal, Bhutan, Bangladesh, Sri Lanka, Afghanistan, and the Maldives depends on traditional non-Western methods. The pattern of education does not include herbal knowledge passed down from generation to generation without any written record. Nor does it include the knowledge of over 20 million indigenous people of India who use 6,000 products from flora and fauna. A number of other countries, such as Malaysia, Indonesia, and Thailand, have assimilated some elements of these natural systems to varying degrees, with knowledge specific to local lore and tradition.

The knowledge of the healing sciences and herbal lore is passed on in all indigenous societies in places as far apart as Malagasy and Tahiti, based on local flora and fauna. These healing practices also address specific needs based on the constitutions of their peoples.

Some remnants of Sushruta[18] and the Arabic systems still survive in the villages of India and other countries. The pahalvans, that is, bodybuilders, wrestlers, and martial artists in the akhadas, have among them expert bonesetters, and, too vast to describe here, the Sino-Japanese-Korean traditions of education in the healing sciences.

The above list of systems is just to show how partial and limited is the information on medical education systems. Once we become aware of the vastness of this topic, we need to attempt to go into the depth of the:

a. education methods whereby such vast knowledge has been passed on for millennia, and

b. The personal philosophy of life imparted to the healer in such texts as the Charaka-samhita (Sharma, 2004)[19] that goes into elaborate details in a live, oral tradition of training disciples not merely in the science but in how to impart that peace of mind without which no disease can be prevented or cured. Those who administer the healing of mind and body in a vast number of traditions are forbidden to ask for a fee, and at the same time, people are culturally trained to give ample offerings.

We need to recognize that such a philosophy of non-commercialization of sciences and services, and the educational methods used to inculcate them, are essential ingredients for a worldwide recipe for peace. That many still choose to lead such non-commercialized lives of "science for service" comes as a surprise to the modern urbanite.

11. Many forms of education, in which the perennial wisdom is translated into a system to fulfill modern needs that have been successfully established in the last century, such as the Montesori system, anthroposophy, Rabindranath Tagore's ideas in Shantiniketan, and the Gandhian schools and colleges. They have produced many citizens and leaders who practice personal, internal peace and social harmony within the fields of their choice and service to others.

12. Lastly, an exceptionally powerful and influential education system that has been followed throughout Hindu-Buddhist Asia (including by the Jainas and others) for nearly 5,000 years. This is known as the gurukula, or Guru's Family. In the ancient Vedic system, a child went to the gurukula (these schools in the forests have been sometimes referred to as "forest academies") to practice a spiritual life, including the study of both the sacred as well as the secular sciences. Here a very strict code of ethics was inculcated together with guidance in cultivating a self-sacrificing, altruistically inclined, peaceful and calm mind. Some teachers, sages, and masters were monks, while others were householders, all dedicated to the philosophy of knowledge for the sake of knowledge and knowledge for the purpose of spiritual liberation (vidyaya' mrtam ashnute being equated with sapientia immortalitatem dat).

The philosophy of nonviolence, so prominent in the culture of India, was developed through the training imparted in these academies. The great Hindu-Buddhist international universities of India, such as Nalanda (10,000 resident students), Taksha-shila (20,000 resident students), and Vikrama-shila, developed out of the same guru-kula tradition.[20] Even now some of the great arts and sciences of India are passed down in a gu-ru-disciple relationship. A student of classical music may live in the fam-ily of his musicguru, whose wife becomes the loco maternis for the disci-ple, feeding him and taking care of him. As in the ancient academies, the true relationship is in knowledge. After receiving the knowledge, at the time of departure, and even throughout life, the disciple makes offerings to the guru family to receive blessings and grace, as well as to help continue the dissemination of "knowledge for the sake of knowledge." Some of the great and famous classical musicians in India, like Ravi Shankar, are products of this system.

There are still a number of functioning gurukulas based on the ancient model that have been modified for modern conditions. Even though some of these have become universities in their own right, while others continue as smaller institutions, the ancient ideals are alive and very much in practice.

Parenting for Peace
This objective consists of the following parts:

1. Training of parents and prospective parents to generate and maintain a calm, peaceful, harmonious, and internally conflict-free mind through:
   a. enacting the ideal of selfless love
   b. contemplative and meditative practices, and mindfulness
   c. learning to reconcile opposites in all contradictions and conflicts as mutually complementary parts of a whole
   d. learning to replace negative emotions such as anger with positive ones such as amity, known as the practice of saumanasya or beautiful-mindedness
   e. forming the habit of reinterpreting negative events and experiences in personal, interpersonal, or inter-group (inter-religious, international, inter-ethnic) relationships into positive ones
   f. reading and learning the traditions of a wide variety of cultures and their histories and personally getting to know their peoples
   g. observing the rituals and sacraments of cultures that are not one's own where the former do not violate the latter.[21]

2. Beauty and sanctity in conception and pregnancy:

a. Reviving the rare and ancient practice of spiritually pre-planned conception. In many cultures, conception is the first life-cycle sacrament. In preparation for this, the would-be parents purify their minds and personalities through guided[22] spiritual practices, as it is understood that the parents not only pass their genes to the child, but also a spark of their own mind-field's luminosity. These spiritual practices will enable the parents' minds and bodies to become fit vessels into which a luminous and peaceful "soul" may be invited, and that child soul's own luminosity may be nurtured.

b. During pregnancy, a calm, peaceful, stress-free environment should be maintained, especially around the mother, in order to give birth to a peaceful citizen. It is well-known in both the traditions and the sciences that the parents,' especially the mother's, state of mind and emotions affect that of the foetus.

   i. work conditions throughout the world need to undergo a radical change for this most important human endeavor, that of bringing peaceful souls into the world. The economic, commercial, and political considerations need to be made subsidiary to this goal.

   ii. Families need to be re-educated to help evoke peaceful feelings in the would-be mother's mind.

c. The would-be mothers should practice filling their minds with peace through:

   i. contemplative practices and mindfulness,

   ii. reading and looking at inspiring stories and pictures,

   iii. undertaking social rituals and ceremonies conducive to these goals of peace.

d. During the nursing period of the child, the same situations need to be maintained and practices observed as during pregnancy.

3. In the period of formal education:

   a. a child needs to understand certain practices conducive to internal peace, identical to the ones recommended for parents, leading to peaceful attitudes and choices in external (social and political) events.

b. the readings and other audio-visual materials for education and entertainment need to include:

    i. texts that teach an altruistic and peaceful personal philosophy,

    ii. stories of inspiring figures from all religions and nations, and

    iii. a re-interpretation of the history of peace where, so far, conflict has been emphasized in the philosophy of history.

c. the ideals need to be inculcated, such as:

    i. "Knowledge is for the sake of knowledge" and success in a vocation and a natural by-product and not the end goal of the same.

    ii. Economics, commerce, finance, and polity are means[23] for maintaining an internal ideal of peace, and their force in life should be curbed to the degree that they are no longer conducive to peace.

    iii. An individual has the will to choose his emotions and ideals, and has the power to live by the same.

d. A child should be given exposure to other nations, religions, and ethnic cultures.

    i. Selections from the works of many religions should be part of the curriculum.

    ii. The child should experience systems of education (only partially listed above) other than the contemporary conventional school system.[24]

4. Just as unjustified violence is a crime against humanity, so also exposing the minds in their formative years to "violence for entertainment" should be declared a crime by an international convention. Many such other methods can be devised by the education guides to have children experience a conflict-free mind and, thereby, eventually create a conflict-free world where peace,

by the definition given in earlier pages, prevails.

We reiterate:

Peace is a state of consciousness and a mind that is free of internal conflict(s) within an individual, as well as collectively within, and consequently among, groups of individuals known as nations, religious or ethnic units, and such other groupings. An education for peace will first aim at creating individuals with conflict-free minds. Only then will a peaceful society emerge.

For this, we propose a conclave of representatives of different types of educational systems in order to formulate detailed curricula of "education for the ethical and peaceful mind."

Let us pray that the minds
of all be educated in the
art of becoming conflict-free
so that peace may prevail.

CHAPTER 9
Social Responsibility in Religions

An area of conduct equally shared by all religions is that of the social responsibility of individuals and groups everywhere. Up to recent times in human history, all matters of human social responsibility were guided by the tenets of and practices within religions.

These include:

- the era known as "enlightenment" in the history of Western philosophy,
- the principle of liberal democracy,
- the development of technology, and
- mass production capitalism and communism that have given rise to mega-police forces on all continents, and have loosened the loyalty people feel toward religion. The concept of social responsibility has been brought into the realm of secular democratic institutions and human rights, separated from the field of religion.

The extent to which this separation has occurred has given an impression to many contemporary sociologists that human social responsibility and human rights are not known or given much importance in religion. In fact, however, it can be safely said that, until recent times, all of human social development took place under the aegis of religion.

Let us look at this topic from several points of view:

1. social responsibility as practiced by the adherents of religion in different areas of life throughout history;

2. the current influence of religion on benevolent social structures;

3. The rules of social responsibility as set out by the scriptures and by the founders of different religions; and

4. the possible continued applications of these rules, to be modified for the future conduct of human responsibility.

I shall include these at different points in the following discussion.

I do not mean to deny the fact that in some areas of life an illogical or extremist interpretation of the principles of religion has led to most irresponsible and destructive behaviors on the part of its practitioners, but a law misinterpreted is not thereby rendered invalid, it only requires a correct interpretation for its just application. Let us look at the way religions have laid down, developed, and enforced human responsibility.

For thousands of years, all social structures were, at least in theory, governed by the tenets of religion. It is only in more recent times that this has changed.

The basic unit of any social structure is the family. Whatever be the definition and mode of marriage, it has always been governed, and is now governed in large part, within the tenets of religion. This includes the rules of partnership between spouses, parents, children, and other relations. It would be a redundant effort to try to prove it otherwise, or even to seek to provide a proof for something so self-evident. The rules of inheritance, though they have changed from time to time, have been guided by texts like the Vedas (Macdonell, Muller, & Oldenberg, 2005), the Qu'ran Sharif (Ali, 1995; Maududi, 1996), the Bible (Holy Bible, 1982), the Laws of Manu (Doniger, 1991),[1] and the principles taught by saints of all faiths, such as the Sikh Gurus. It is religion that has forbidden incestuous relations as well as libidinous inter-sexual behaviors. The laws of the lands laid down by the state worldwide have only validated and enforced what was taught by religion.

The family circle established by religious teachings expands into the relationships within neighbourhoods. "Love thy neighbor" is a religious teaching, either explicitly stated or implicit in the teachings of all religions. This sense of social responsibility has always been firmly established by religion.

However much some of us may disagree with some of the principles and rules espoused by Manu and Mitakshara (Mishra, 2002),[2] the Shari'at (Kamali, 2008), or the Books of Deuteronomy and Leviticus (in the Bible), the fact remains that the laws laid down therein governed the society for many millennia, and they helped maintain stable social structures. We do not mean to gainsay the fact that now the secular laws are fulfilling the same purpose of stability, but a large number of secular social laws still have their historical roots in religion.

Many of the areas of social life, such as governance in villages or in entire kingdoms, were guided by religious texts and preceptors throughout history. Even though many of these realms are now separated from the field of religion, their historical roots in religion, once again, cannot be denied. Who can deny, for example, the mental and symbolical connection between the holy "panj piyare"[3] and the five impartial judges in the panchayat[4] system of secular governance?

In all religions, human conduct has been guided on the basis of the duty to:

- govern oneself, and then
- to extend that governance to an ever-enlarging circle of family, neighborhood, village, nation, and the earth.

The principles of self-governance are well known, primary examples being:

- amity
- nonviolence
- freedom from avarice and greed
- control over anger and jealousy

- charity and sharing of one's worldly goods with those revered or those less fortunate
- control over base passions.

No religion disagrees with any of these guidelines to life. When translated into a social structure, the practical application of these principles forms a base for responsible human conduct in society.

For example, the principle of amity governs the rules laid down for the conduct of war in a just manner, and the kindly treatment of a defeated enemy—as seen in texts such as the Laws of Manu and the Mahabharata (Narasimhan, 1965).

We may disagree, as many of us do, with capital punishment today as retribution for a murder, but the fact remains that we all agree with the religious commandment "thou shalt not kill" as taught in whatever language, century, or religion.

If we followed the advice that one should not answer a neighbor's anger with anger, but with tolerance and understanding, that would do away with some of the work of the police forces.

It is the greed of the few (individuals, corporations, and nations) that impoverishes so many on this earth. If we followed the religious precepts that one should:

- conquer greed,
- not take from nature more than one's immediate need, and
- share one's wealth with those we revere or those who are less fortunate than we,

both our environmental problems as well as poverty would be significantly reduced. Only those who are not aware of their human social responsibility neglect to follow these sacred precepts.

Have these precepts of human social responsibility ever been followed? Given that human beings are imperfect, these teachings have seldom been practiced in their entirety, but the evidence is before our eyes to prove that there has been a large-scale adherence to these principles throughout history.

It was through his religious inspiration that Amenhotep IV (Akhenaton), the 13th century B.C. Egyptian pharaoh, dismantled his armies.

It was under the guidance of the Indian gymnosophists (as referred to by the historians Plutarch and Pliny) that Alexander the marauder from Macedonia finally refrained from using war as an instrument of imperial expansion.

It was due to religious inspiration that emperor Ashoka abstained from developing the instruments of war and established hospices, orchards, monasteries, and so forth.

It was because of the teachings of a Taoist master that Changiz Khan finally turned away from war.

A great preceptor such as Guru Nanak, he of the hallowed name, the founder of the Sikh faith, exhibited the folly of exploitative capital when he squeezed the delicious foods of a greedy rich man and showed that these foods dripped with blood (of the innocent poor) but that a poor man's dried bread was purer and fit to eat.

For thousands of years, followers of many religions have been taught to give dashaansh, a tenth part of one's income (tithing in the Christian tradition), to the holy and the poor. The same principle is found in zakat, one of the five duties of every Muslim. And numerous religious communities maintain charity chests for the benefit of the needy.

The Christian saints are known for their service to the leprosy patients who were discarded by the society in medieval Europe, as also in India. Many people of faith outside Christianity, such as the late Baba Amte, gave the best years of their lives in service of these afflicted ones. Also in medieval Europe, in that widely impoverished society, the churches and monasteries were known for feeding and serving the poor, and many still run soup kitchens and night shelters for the poor even in cities like New York.

It is a common sight at the Hindu places of pilgrimage that well-to-do pilgrims feed crowds of hundreds of hungry people and distribute clothes and blankets to them. The Sikh Gurudwaras[5] lead in setting an example in service of the poor and the needy with their 24-hour langars (free food offerings) to all who would drop in. They also set an example of equality in society from centuries before the ideals of "liberty, equality, and fraternity" espoused by French social philosophers were enshrined in the state-craft of many lands.

Not only kings, but all who could afford it, have always built hospices, dharma-shalas (pilgrim rest houses), waterwells (kuaan), stepwells (baoris), and reservoirs for the benefit of the traveler, the sick, and the agriculturist. These are all examplesof human social responsibility as taught in religion.

Many religious communities and well-to-do individuals used to leave bageechees (orchards) for the common use of all. Alas, under the present, not very religious, society, these facilities have all but disappeared. But have they?

Many of these institutions still survive. At a time when India, China, and Africa are suffering from increasing encroachments of deserts, it is because of the continued diligent practice of the precepts of the Bishnoi religion that many areas in the middle of the deserts of Rajasthan remain green where many wild species flourish. For hundreds of such examples of the preservation of forests through religious practices, see Malhotra (2007).

Religion has provided education to millions throughout history. The temples and monasteries of India, Tibet, China, and Europe, the Gurud-waras and mosques, often had their attached patha-shala schools and ma-darsas. Almost the entire educational system of Thailand is run by the Buddhist monks.

Many of these institutions have changed their forms. In the ancient history of India, the temples often had hospitals associated with them, hospitals not only for humans but for the birds and beasts as well. Until today, thousands come to the ashrams run by the saintly to seek healing for their illnesses.

Many well-established temples and guru-dwaras run school lunch programs whereby hundreds of thousands of children are fed in many cities.

The religious organizations run huge hospitals, charity programs, and schools and colleges. The chain of Khalsa colleges and Dayanand Anglo Vedic (DAV) colleges are well known in North India. The great temples of South India, like Tirupati, run large universities. The spirit continues as the forms have undergone a change of scale.

Several other points need to be borne in mind in this discussion.

There is no doubt that the social systems have changed, but the principles are perennial. It is when we abandon these perennial principles that our contemporary social structures suffer the onslaught of unethical, violent, greedy, and destructive behavior. For example, let us remember the story of one of the maharajas of Patiala who enjoined his palanquin-bearers to carry the palanquin of a venerated learned man. Today's "kings," those who have "democratically" replaced the kings of yore, do not even dream of such acts of humility and reverence. Consequently, the respect for knowledge for the sake of knowledge has all but vanished, and the principal of a college is a humble servant before the minister, and no longer his mentor. Then who is there to teach the minister to remain free of corruption out of an adherence to some spiritual principle?

It is the religious texts that enjoined the course of training for princes and laid down the qualities of ministers. The training prescribed for the princes in the texts (see the Laws of Manu; Chanakya [Srikantan, 2007]; Mahabharata), whereby they may take care of their subjects in humility and self-sacrifice, and with wisdom and justice, is required for the government officials of today, but it is no longer available in a non-religious social structure. Here are the qualities of the king as enjoined in the religious texts:

> patient, tolerant…eager to listen, learned, intuitive, controlled, always pleasant speakers, forgiving in case of transgressions, not excessively contradicting [others], doing work, filled with sacred faith and devotion… giving a hand to the distressed, having wise ministers…not saying "I"…non-arrogant, always with a pleasant face, protector…non-angry, having a beautifully high mind… watching over the citizens' well-being…
>
> MAHABHARATA (118.28-33)

Let us look at the qualities of the ministers prescribed in the same texts:

> …well-educated…expert at theory and experiential knowledge, master of the depths of meanings of all sciences

147

and texts, tolerant...grateful, powerful, forgiving, controlled, master of [one's] senses, not greedy...well-wisher [for all]...not arrogant...soft-spoken, patient.

MAHABHARATA (118.18-25)

When those socially responsible follow such precepts, they have the capacity to create a society of citizens with a high "happiness quotient," a term invented by the King Wangchuk of Bhutan, who has developed the notion of a "national happiness quotient" on the basis of his strong religious belief in Buddhist precepts.

A question arises: are we going to remain satisfied with the fact that "being religious, we give charity to the poor?" Does religion have anything to offer for eliminating the causes of poverty? Here we need to undertake massive research enterprises, intellectual discussions, and conferences—a whole new movement towards a vigorous investigation of truth in these regards.

1. Detailed sociological studies need to be undertaken to research:
   - the pivotal role played by religious precepts in cultivating the positive elements of social responsibility, as well as
   - where it has played a negative role, and
   - how the negative may be replaced by positive elements, and
   - where, in legal and political histories of the world, and in the contemporary legal and socio-political structures of societies, the current secular forms are continuations from the religious precepts and laws, and
   - where the discontinuity of these are beneficial or detrimental to social harmony, peace, and the prosperity of all.

2. How we may interpret the religious precepts so that they may be applied to offer solutions to contemporary problems such as:
   - war and peace,
   - inter-religious harmony,
   - equitable distribution of wealth and power to eliminate poverty and exploitation (as done by the Christian thinkers of what is

known as "liberation theology"), in other words, a full, modern theory of the religious-spiritual teaching of economics by renunciation, and

- spiritually motivated altruistic (non-commercial) and ethical ways to save the planet from environmental degradation and gradual disintegration.

Let us hope that some religiously motivated philanthropists can offer to finance the above suggested research projects at any university willing to undertake such an endeavor.

Let us further pray that the perennial continues to prevail to nourish and guide all the inevitable changes that must occur through the successive "modern" and "postmodern" times of the future centuries.

CHAPTER 10
Proposals for Peace

Based on the facts and discussions presented in the preceding chapters, what follows are both foundational thoughts and practical proposals offered to the World Peace Summit of Leaders in Religion and Spirituality.

It is heartening to see that the possible role of religion and spirituality in bringing peace to the world is being acknowledged through current efforts at the United Nations. To change that possibility into reality, the following proposals need to be accepted and presented.

In teaching the history of humanity in all parts of the world, the developments of political and economic power alone have been emphasized. The developments in religion have been included only as adjuncts to political and economic power.

Only disputes between religions are brought into focus, presenting religion as a cause of strife. The role played by pure spirituality within religions in establishing harmony and conciliation has not been emphasized.

Thus, the entire methodology of teaching the role of religion needs to be examined, and a new approach to this methodology needs to be internationally established to present a picture that can be a source of inspiration toward peace, equity, and justice. In studying the unifying streams in religion, we would arrive at a world history of peace through religion and spirituality, and would be able to inspire future generations through examples from the past.

Be it proposed that:

- The methodology as currently adopted in teaching the role of religion and spirituality in history be thoroughly re-examined by a scholarly body of those well versed in all aspects of religion.

- the teaching concerning the role of religion in history be based on the premise that, at the levels of both the common people and the spiritual teachers, rather than solely at the level of the politically powerful, more often than not, religion has played an important role in helping to develop some wise, peaceful, and conciliatory solutions to human problems and to the overall human quest.

In the study of comparative religion and of specific theologies, teachers often do not take into account what the particular beliefs and practices of religions actually mean to the followers of a given religion. This is especially true of the way Eastern religions—their belief systems, practices, and historical developments, are explained and interpreted in theological and academic institutions—and other podiums in Western countries.

It is, therefore, proposed that:

- all teaching concerning a religion should primarily be imparted by learned and qualified followers of that religion. This is the only way that the followers of various religions will understand each other's points of view. Through the mutual understanding generated by adopting this course, the various religions will become effective instruments of peace.

Be it further proposed that:

- The methods adopted by various religions for proselytizing should be examined by an impartial, international, inter-religious commission that would find and suggest ways in which the religions may propagate themselves without causing hurt and violence, without force, fraud, or economic or political coercion, and, yet,
- preserve each religion's freedom of speech and expression.
- The leaders of all religions agree to enjoin upon their

adherents to refrain from criticizing other religions, while
- maintaining freedom of expression by stating their own belief systems in an emphatically positive tone.

Recognizing that certain practices of the contemplative path are common to the followers of all religions, and that with some modifications, these can also be practiced by those who do not hold a belief in God or religion, be it proposed that all deliberations of the world councils:

- shall begin with such a common, contemplative experience in silence, and
- shall emphasize that all departments of education and institutions of knowledge encourage their students and teachers to train the mind to trigger a peaceful state at will by applying the same contemplative methods.

Formal Proposal One

Be it resolved that a World Council of Ethics and Peace be established under the aegis of the United Nations, UNESCO, and leading interfaith organizations composed of:

1. Representatives of all religions and belief systems that recognize the need for education regarding ethical conduct and peace;

2. All leaders worldwide of the different movements for nonviolent change;

3. Nobel Laureates who have received the Nobel Prize for peace;

4. Academicians in the field of Peace Studies, including philosophers, poets, and artists who have significantly advanced ideas of ethical conduct and peace;

With the purpose and objectives to:

1. Advise all organs of the United Nations, and states and political entities, on questions of morality and ethics relating to sovereignty, constitutionality, human rights, human relationships, equitable distribution of wealth and opportunity, relationships among religions and ethnic entities, environmental issues, and such other matters of common interest to humanity;

2. Plan for the education for peace to be successful in all nations, through all systems of education;
   a. Advise nations and their leaders on helping to establish and maintain an ethical and peaceful world order;
   b. Serve as arbitration counselors, mediators, and facilitators in situations of continuing or impending conflicts among any entities, whether existing de jure or de facto, without prejudice to the principle of sovereignty of any party in dispute;
   c. Continue to develop, define, clarify, and advance the world's consciousness of a philosophy and methodology for peace and nonviolent progress for all.

To achieve these results through a multilateral organization, the charter may be:
   a. Drafted and proposed by a group dedicated to these ideals;
   b. Passed in the first assembly of the World Council of Ethics and Peace, as well as in the various organs of the United Nations.

Formal Proposal Two
Bearing in mind the definition that:

Peace is a state of consciousness and mind that is free of internal conflicts within an individual, as well as collectively within, and consequently among, groups of individuals known as families, nations, religions, or ethnic units,
And that:

Education for ethical conduct and peace in a planet-wide system will consist of:

1. Imprinting minds so that they hold a holistic view of all human experience (memory, histories, traditions), thought, and belief systems as constituents of a single whole;

2. Facilitating all imprinting that leads to freedom from conflict within an individual mind, and consequently among social, ethnic, religious, national, or any other groupings.

Be it resolved that all organs of the United Nations, as well as all states and political entities, enter into an international "Covenant for Education and Parenting for Ethical Conduct and Peace" wherein, among other supporting steps to be drafted, the following primary objectives be stated:

1. That the condemnation of any religion or ethnic entity be considered a violation of human rights;

2. That any display of "violence for entertainment" be declared a crime against humanity;

3. That human history, in accordance with a new philosophy of history, be taught as a history of peace in which violent conflict is presented as an aberration and a violation of the natural human urge for peace and harmony;

4. That popular as well as academic works, comics, or storybooks, whether in printed or electronic form, be made available to populations worldwide, and in their own languages, depicting the:
   a. Positive and peaceful elements of various religions and ethnic cultures;
   b. Life stories of saints and the saintly, the noble spiritual guides, leaders in peace, and founders and high proponents of altruistic, ethical, and philosophical systems based on the

values of self-sacrificing love and harmony;

5. That the educational systems teach widely, from preschool level to advanced studies, the history, philosophy, and practical steps of non-aggressive conflict resolution in internal, interpersonal, and inter-group (inter-religious, inter-state, inter-ethnic) situations;

6. That concrete proposals be developed within a reasonable time period whereby the economic, commercial, educational, and professional structures, work organizations, and work ethics, provide ample opportunities to parents worldwide to enable them to pass on the values of love, harmony, peace, and other ethical values in daily conduct to children. By thus rendering the minds of the children psychologically and spiritually conflict free, this would preclude the possibilities of the leaders and populace of future generations inflicting the collective neurosis and aberration of war on fellow human beings.

Be it further resolved that as support that is parallel to the endeavors required to achieve the above objectives:

The entire global community be given the opportunity to benefit from the wide spectrum of experience of the numerous educational systems that have prevailed in many traditions worldwide by having a conclave of:

    a. representatives of different types of educational systems, and
    b. the departments of Peace Studies in academic institutions be invited, preferably through UNESCO, the United Nation's University campuses, and leading interfaith organizations, with the purpose of developing:
       i. a theory of education and parenting for ethical conduct and peace, drawing upon the millennia-old experience of the traditions of peace education, and assimilating their most positive and agreeable points into a comprehensive scheme;
      ii. a worldwide plan for a system of education for ethical conduct and peace;

iii. the practical steps for establishing such a system, including the curricula of "education for the ethical and peaceful mind."

Religion for Preventing Terrorism

The following resolution was presented in a meeting organized by the World Council of Religious Leaders in Dag Hammersjkold Hall of the United Nations, as a recommendation to the Secretary General of the United Nations, on May 21, 2003.

Being aware that fear and aggression are primarily mental events, only a terrorized mind can, consequently, terrorize others. This insight takes into account that individual and collective events occur as part of historical forces, developed over centuries and millennia, in which all parties have been participants in a continuous chain of actions and reactions.

Based on the fact that in the sacred books of all religions, there are commandments and admonitions that equally encourage us to take to the path of non-aggression, meekness, love, tolerance, and forgiveness, these truths are held self-evident by the adherents of all religions, many practices being common to the followers of all religions.

Re-establishing that the practice of making derogatory statements concerning other religions and ethnic groups, being contrary to the above principles of harmony, is a violation both of divine will that is good and benevolent toward all living beings, and of the basic human rights to live in peace and prosperity.

When the teachings of love have been successfully applied in interpersonal and inter-societal relationships, there is profuse evidence that, for societies with religions that have professed these teachings, large geographical areas of the earth for long periods of time have had no inter-religious strife, although such strife occurred frequently elsewhere. Such religions also recognized the power and practice of confession and forgiveness as common spiritual and ethical principles.

Be it resolved that the participants of this meeting of the World Council of Religious Leaders unanimously agree among themselves, and herewith recommend to the Secretary General of the United Nations:

1. That a study and research program, with the dissemination of its outcomes, be instituted:
    a. to look into the forces that historically brought about the success of the teachings of non-aggression, love, and tolerance where such has been evident in the various periods and geographical areas of human history;
    b. to find ways for consciously implementing the patterns of such forces in our times;

2. That the scholars and theologians of all religions categorically state that the admonitions to aggression against non-adherents are to be interpreted only as indicating an internal struggle toward the Good within a human being, and that such aggression not be directed against another individual or group;

3. That the supreme leaders and councils of all religions advise their adherents to totally refrain from condemnation of others' belief systems;

4. That the leaders and authoritative councils of various religions find ways for seeking and extending forgiveness in order to support and deepen the mutual understanding and harmonious relationships in the present, in order to lay a foundation for universal inter-religious harmony in the future;

5. That as a natural accompaniment to the resolve to undertake and encourage such studies, as well as acts of mutual forgiveness and harmony, the participants of this meeting of the World Council of Religious Leaders:
    a. strongly influence and encourage political entities, whether they are in power de facto or de jure, to prevent all such vocal or physical acts that violate the teachings of nonviolence and that cause hurt or harm to individuals and groups of the adherents of other religions and societies;
    b. persuade all in the field of various systems of education that:

i. the teachings imparted regarding other religions should be done so only by the adherents of the particular religion, and not by those who are unsympathetic to the same;

ii. the teaching of the principles, and the history of non violence and the methods thereof, be made an essential part of the school and college curricula;

iii. in this context, to declare all acts of terrorism as violations of religious edicts and of human rights;

6. That through such positive scholarly, educational, and spiritual endeavors, all of humanity be spared the scourge of intolerance, mutual condemnation, persecution, oppression, and terrorism.

The Council of World Religious Leaders further recommends to the Secretary General that the United Nations General Assembly adopt such a declaration of mutual respect among religions as an article of faith common to all of humanity.

Footnotes

Preface:

1. Let us read "country" to mean "planet", echoing the sanyasins' (Hindu monks') prayer: sva-desho bhuvana-trayam, "my country is the three worlds."
2. In linguistic history, the word "man" means a contemplative being.
3. Greek for Earth Mother; cognate to the Sanskrit "go"—nominative singular "gauh," the Earth identified as the ever-milk-giving cow; the idea of a living motherly entity, a live deity, sacred and ever-loving to all.

Chapter 1:

1. Kuang Yin—Mother Divine, the Lady in Compassion in China. Known as Dolma in Tibet, Kwannon in Japan, Tara in India.
2. Two aspects of the Divine Mother in India: Lakshmi, the Mother of prosperity, fortune, and success, and Saraswati, the Mother of wisdom, knowledge, intuition, inspiration, music, and the arts. Both, to the yogis, are powers of the inner spiritual Force known as kundalini.
3. Mala—Hindu-Buddhist rosary; tasbeeh—the Muslim rosary.
4. Zam-Zam, the sacred stream where the Haj (Muslim pilgrimage to Mecca) pilgrims touch the sacred water and bring some of the water home.
5. Chilla is a practice of Sufi saints consisting of particular ascetic and purificatory endeavors and non stop, sleepless prayer for forty days.
6. Kadazan is one of the indigenous nations of Borneo whose wise men also undertake purificatory practices during solitary stays in the forest.
7. Qur'an, holy book of the Muslims.
8. Mahabharata of India is one of the world's largest epics consisting of 100,000 verses detailing the stories of the rise and fall of dynasties through interactions of the cosmic-spiritual with the personal, and of the celestial with the terrestrial.
9. Dhammapada is the most popular collection of the Budhha's sayings; it is read by every Buddhist.
10. Avesta is the holy book of the Mazda-yasnians, the followers of Zarathushtra.

11. The Upanishads are the ancient texts of India regarding the direct experience of the metaphysical form.

12. Proto-pashupati, a sculpture with many features resembling the later sculptures of Shiva seated in meditation. Quite independently, a cauldron excavated near Gundestrup in Denmark has similar features carved on its surface.

13. Mohen-jo-daro (literally, hillock of the dead) in the Sindh province of what is now Pakistan, where the remains of the most ancient proto-Indian civilization have been excavated, with well-planned cities having covered drainage, public baths, and magnificent sculptures. The script has not yet been deciphered.

14. Vestal virgins are the virgin priestesses who served the goddess Vestain Rome, the keeper of the sacred fire hearth of the Roman civilization. Saraswati, see footnote No. 2 above.

15. Saraswati, see footnote No. 2 above.

16. Oneida is one of the American "Indian" nations that was a major participant in the Confederation of Nations created by Hiawatha.

17. Kumari are the several living virgin deities of Nepal who are consecrated to that position from the ages of two or three.

18. Naga is the Hindu snake deity. Follows the tradition of using symbols to interpret life at various levels.

19. Shiva is one of the components of the Hindu triune God, He of creation, preservation, and dissolution of the universe. Shiva is the presiding divine Force of dissolution as well as of meditation.

20. Krishna is one of many forms in which God becomes flesh; the teacher of the Bhagavad Gita (the Song Celestial).

21. Kaliya is the hundred-headed naga that terrified the people of the Vraj country; Krishna danced on his head and finally banished him to the underworld.

22. Rama is one of the many forms in which God becomes flesh; Hero of the Ramayana story. Lakshmana is Rama's loyal and obedient younger brother.

23. Hasan and Husain are heroes in the Shia branch of Islam in the battles of succession to Prophet Mohammad. They are inspiring examples of self-sacrifice for God.

24. Form of Muslim song popular in South Asia that is full of utter devotion, inspiration, and divine fervor. Both Hindus and Muslims equally enjoy immersing themselves in its devotional nature.

25. A very popular sacred festival in India in honor of Durga, the form of Mother Divine that is fiercely protective of her devotees.

26. Yajna is the worship performed with burnt offerings being tossed into the fire; this is a very common form of private and public worship in India.

27. Worship.

28. Festival celebrating the conquest of good over evil.

29. Prasad refers to the sweet and fruit offerings that are placed before an icon that is being worshipped; they are distributed to devotees at the end of the ceremony as "grace" emanating from the divine figure.

30. Followers of the Jain religion, established by a succession of 24 holy founders, the last of whom was Mahavira, a contemporary of the Buddha. The religion, holding nonviolence and asceticism in its highest regard, is difficult for average people to follow; it did not become known as widely as Buddhism, but its depth and philosophical scope is unimaginably immense.

31. Hymns in the languages of India.

32. A devotional saint who composed a version of the Ramayana epic in the spoken language of the people; this is the most popular form of the sacred epic in North India. Mothers sing its verses to children as lullabies to create a divine impression on their minds; hundreds of thousands may gather to listen to its recitation, sitting enraptured all night.

33. A very ancient and complex classical style of vocal music.

34. Odin and Thor, Nordic gods of light and thunder.

35. The West African nation from which a large number of people were brought as slaves to America. Their deities go by the generic name Orixa. The Santeria and Condamble religions of Cuba and the Bahia are combinations of Christian and traditional African religions.

36. Ascetic mendicant, a well-known phenomenon in South Asia.

37. Kami is the Nature deities of the Japanese religion. At the head is Ama-terasu, Mother Sun, to whom the emperors trace their ancestry.

38. Narayana is the Divine Spirit that meditates on the waters (com-

pare to Genesis, Chapter 1, Verse 2). Ganesha, the popular elephant-headed deity of India, God as the remover of obstacles and source of stability.

39. Agama-tirtha, literally "that which has come from the sacred country," the Balinese name for what in India is called Hinduism.

40. Pre-Hindu-Buddhist Balinese religion.

41. A leading hero of the epic Mahabharata to whom Krishna the God-Incarnate imparted the knowledge known as the Bhagavad Gita (Song of the Blessed One).

42. Sankhya is the system of philosophy that provides definitions and categories that are then used in yoga for physical and spiritual practicums. Yoga philosophy cannot be understood without understanding the formal system of Sankhya, hence the two are often referred to as Sankhya-yoga.

43. Dharma is a concept central to all religions that were founded in India, such as Vedic-Hinduism, Buddhism, Jainism, and Sikhism. It is the very Nature of divinity in the universe that a human being must manifest in him or herself in his/her thoughts, words, and deeds, personal or socio-politico-economic. Its level of observation in each individual or group is according to their spiritual station and the level of their spiritual realization.

44. Harshavardhana was the Indian emperor in the Seventh century A.D. who granted equal respect to the spiritual guides of all religions. He also gave patronage and honor to Xuan-Zang who, under the patronage of the T'ang emperors in Ch'ang-An (the capital of China), traversed the silk road to India, studied and taught at the then famous Nalanda university, took 600 sacred texts to China, and trained the scholarly monks to translate the same into Chinese. These are the standard Chinese Buddhist texts studied and recited to this day

45. Kshatriya is the second one of the four divisions of society in India, the administrative and soldier group, including the royal lineage.

46. The Vajji and Licchavi nations formed democratic republics. The remnants of their Sixth century B.C. legislative assembly can be seen at the small city of Vaishali, a little distance from Patna, the modern capital of India's Bihar state.

47. The sangomas are the wise elders and spiritual guides of the Zulu

tradition; the most famous at the present time is Credo Mutwa, author of numerous well-known works.

48. Bishnoi is a 400-year old religion in India whose followers adhere to 29 principles including total nonviolence and nonviolation of all of nature, including living beings. Theirs are the greenest villages in the desert of Rajasthan. On the boundary of the village are troughs for wild animals to drink from, and food is also left here. They do not permit a single tree to be cut. They have been ecofriendly to this extent for the past four centuries.

49. A movement started by mountain women of the Garhwal region of the Himalayas in North India. When the loggers came from the plains, they were accorded the traditional mountain hospitality, but then when the loggers entered the forests to cut the trees, the women and children clung to the trees, hugging them. The loggers, not wishing to commit murder, left the trees alone. Thus was born the Chipko (Cling!) movement that set an example for the protectors of the environment everywhere to follow.

50. Popol Vuh. After the Spanish conquistadores destroyed the Mayan civilization and its books, this is one sacred book that has survived.

51. Rig Veda. One of the four Vedas that are the most ancient books of the human library, still recited mnemonically. They form the historical foundation of all of the religions and philosophies of India.

52. Mimamsa. One of the six major schools of Indian Hindu-Vedic philosophy. It explains and discusses (a) the origin of inspired knowledge, and (b) the acts of worship and ritual. In the context of the acts, it established the philosophy of karma. This system is also known as purvamimamsa, the "prior mimamsa," as contrasted with uttara-mimamsa, the "latter mimamsa," that is the non-ritualistic, contemplative Vedanta.53. Brahma-jala-sutta is one of the texts in the voluminous sacred Buddhist canon.

54. Vishu-rupa—see above. Vi-bhuti is the vast variety of the manifestations of divine power.

55. For a deeper understanding of this concept, see Ranjan (2008).

56. Two of the greatest scholar-saints of the Jain tradition.

Chapter 2:

1. Muharram is a well-known commemoration observed by Shia Muslims in memory of the martyred brothers Hasan and Husain.

2. There are two Eid festivals in an Islamic year: Eid-ul-Adha, commemorating Abraham's readiness to sacrifice his son to God, and Eid-ul-Fitr, celebrated immediately after the completion of the fasting month of Ramzan.

3. Divali is the popular Hindu festival of lights.

4. Iftar is the dinner with which the daily fast in the month of Ramzan is ended.

5. The Hanuman-chalisa is a forty-verse composition in praise of Hanuman, the devotee par excellence, sung by millions of Hindus throughout northern India.

6. Dargah is the holy grave of a Muslim saint.

7. Mazdayasnian is the correct name for the followers of Zarathushtra (Zoroaster)—they who offer worship to God as Ahur Mazda, the Great Force of Universal Light.

8. The Tirthankaras are the 24 founders of the Jain religion.

9. The names of ceremonies whereby the Jewish, Hindu, and Mazdayasnian young children, usually boys, are granted entry into the study of the holy scriptures of their respective faiths.

10. Samadhi is the highest goal of yoga meditation systems—the pure, divine consciousness unadulterated by exterior faculties such as the mind.

11. Kashi (and similar concepts in many different spiritual traditions) is the concept that holy cities on earth are only poor projections of their real heavenly counterparts. In India, Kashi (Varanasi) and Go-loka, the pasturelands where Krishna flourished and frolicked, are two examples (there are many others). This concept is not limited to cities alone. The Kailasha mountain (sacred to adherents of three religions) also is in the same category.

12. Gathas are verses directly revealed by God (Ahura Mazda) to Zarathushtra.

13. This shows the progression of the word, from Sanskrit dhyana (meditation) to Pali (the language that the Buddha spoke) jhana, to Chinese Ch'an, to Korean Son, and then to the Japanese Zen.

14. The Holy Book of the Sikhs, a religion of thirty million followers, founded by a succession of ten gurus. The text was finalized 400 years ago and consists of 6,000 divinely inspired songs/psalms divided into chapters by melodies (ragas of Indian music). The first founder of the religion was the exceptionally holy saint Nanak. The tenth guru declared that after him, the holy book alone will be the guru. The holy book is enshrined in all guru-dwaras (doors to the guru's mansion), as the temples of the Sikh faith are called.

15. The prayer that is recited five times a day enjoined upon a Muslim, Namaz in the Iranian tradition, salat in the Arabic.

16. Khanqah is the Sufi center of meditation. Zen-do is the Zen meditation center.

17. The common Hindu confessional prayer is: papo'ham papa-karmaaham papatma papa-sambhavah; trahi mam pundarikaksha sarva-papa-haro harih. I am sinful. [I am of] sinful actions. [I am] the very self of sin, born in sin. Protect me, oh Lotus-eyed One. [Verily] the Lord is the remover of all sins.

18. Khurd-Avesta, or "short Avesta," is the Mazdayasnian book of ritual and liturgy commonly used in India.

19. Svastika, an ancient graphic sign of many cultures on all continents, expressing many layers of meaning. For example, in the ancient Mayan culture of what is now known as Guatemala and Yucatan, it means the end of one phase and the beginning of another.

20. Bindu is one of the fundamental concepts in the philosophy of Tantra. The universe begins from a bindu (a word cognate to the English word point, the German punkt), a dot of light, and returns to the same. So, also, each field of material, mental, or spiritual energy has a still point in its center, of which it is an expansion, and into which it is withdrawn when meditation is successful. The Sufi equivalent is nuqteh, the Arabic word for the same concept.

21. Vipassana ("mindfulness," "observation") is the practice of meditation as taught in the Southern Buddhist schools in Myanmar, Thailand, Laos, and others. The Northern Buddhist schools (e.g., the Tibetan) include the precepts of vipassana, but also have a vast variety of other meditations not acceptable to Southern meditation guides.

22. Preksha-dhyana is a meditation utilizing mindfulness and observation as taught by the contemporary Jain meditation guides.

23. Dhikr refers to Sufi meditation practices that include the remembrance of a name of God while feeling the flow of breath.

24. Hesychia is the path of stillness taught by the Greek Orthodox and Russian Orthodox masters, known as the startsi (singular staretz). Its primary text is the Philokalia in Greek, or Dobrotilubye in Russian. Its major practice is mentally reciting the Jesus prayer or the Lord's prayer with the observation of breath flow.

Chapter 3:

1. *God* by Usharbudh Arya (1979) (now Swami Veda Bharati).

2. *Bhishma: Introducing Mahabharata* by Swami Veda Bharati (2002b).

3. The concept is annunciated in sankalpa, the statement of space, time, and identity in the beginning of every Hindu ceremony. For a brief paraphrase, see Veda Bharati (1997).

4. There are two versions of that verse: tadatmanam, "then, my Self," is the vulgate version. But in the Kashmir version of the Bhagavad Gita, the verse reads tadatmansham, "then, a particle of my Self." A version from the lesser known Kashmir recitation is chosen here.

5. Pir, the sufi Master and spiritual guide. Murid, the disciple.

6. Those who propagate the "conflict of civilizations", juxtaposing the "Christian" God against Allah, may not have been informed that Christian liturgies in the Arabic-speaking countries universally use the word Allah for the "Christian God." One wonders if the polymorphous monotheism of the Egyptians and the Ptolemies did not somehow seep into the Coptic traditions, thus rendering many people of that region tolerant of other names of God. It is worth investigating.

7. Some years ago, the members of a particular church in Michigan were burning bibles with a declaration that only the King James version was true and authentic, and all others should be destroyed (*Detroit News*, 2003).

Chapter 4:

1. This was a lecture presented at the Fifth International Conference of Chief Justices of the World, organized by the World Unity and Peace Department, City Montessori School, Lucknow, India, December, 2004.

2. See Veda Bharati (2000).

3. See Buhler (1964).

4. See Veda Bharati (2002b).

5. Unfortunately, Kashmir remains a festering sore. The ex-king, known as a philosopher-king, was a presidential candidate in the last Indian election.

6. For an array of references in the ancient law books of India that prohibit the king from being a lawmaker, and enjoin him to protect and implement the vast diversities of common laws, please see Kane (1941). It would be interesting to research notes on case laws, if any survive, from thedifferent states.

7. The Malaysian model is, in my view, the perfect solution to the Israel/Palestine problem, where similarly parallel systems of law can be practiced, with Jews living in a Jewish state and Palestinians in a Muslim/Christian state.

8. See www.pbs.org/wgbh/pages/frontline/shows/mandela/boy/stenel/html.

9. See Ramos (2000). Drawing on his days in the classrooms of M.I.T. and on the playing fields of Ghana, the U.N. leader pursues a moral vision for enforcing world peace.

10. Excluding landlocked Nepal, whose relationship with the British rulers of India was in a class of its own.

11. We can cite numerous examples from texts on polity and ethics in the Hindu, Jain, and Buddhist traditions, as well as historical evidence, to support these statements. This would require a lengthy treatise that may be undertaken by students studying theory and history of the relationship between philosophy and the state. Such dissertations should also analyze the causes of any failures suffered by those who teach the philosophy of renunciation.

12. See the Bhagavad Gita 2.62ff; see Veda Bharati (2001), sutras 2.7-9.

13. See Lutz, Greischar, Rawlings, Ricard, & Davidson (2004).

14. We use the word Socratic to include other, similar philosophers, such as the Shramanas, Brahmins, Taoist philosophers, and Sangomas.

Chapter 5:

1. Stories of the Buddha's past lives that detail his evolution toward enlightenment.

2. Shakti, potentia, makes the Lord omnipotent. It is in its cosmic inception as maya, God's creative power, that all that was concealed in the transcendental Brahman is made manifest.

3. Om, the supreme name of God that, even when pronounced, remains unpronounced until its concealed half mora of consciousness is wordlessly and soundlessly experienced in the state of samadhi. The Upanishads state that God is the unspoken speaker within us all.

Chapter 6:

1. Hindus have contributed to building mosques in recent times on the Indian subcontinent. At this time, the Sikhs of India and Pakistan, who are doing kar seva, giving as a labor of love, are renovating Nankana Sahib. They are being joined by Pakistani Muslims

Chapter 8:

1. This definition serves as a comprehensive compromise among views held by various schools of neurology, as well as those of the philosophy of consciousness.

2. Nepal and Japan have been omitted, as they are both politically very different cases.

3. With the exception of Kashmir, whose ex-king, the philosopher Dr. Karan Singh, is a leading figure in interfaith dialogue as well as a prominent statesman in democratic India.

4. For example, the author learned to speak Italian in one night by employing the method of yoga-nidra.

5. My spiritual guide, Swami Rama, demonstrated in psycho-physiological research laboratories his ability to produce alpha, theta, and delta brain waves at will, and to control his autogenic states. See the *Encyclopaedia Britannica Science Supplement,* 1973.

6. Lorikayan, also known as Chanaini. A folk epic sung widely in the Eastern part of Uttar Pradesh and the Bihar states of India, as well in major parts of the Indian Diaspora; it has versions in a number of Eastern dialects of medieval Hindi such as Magahi, Avadhi, Bhojpuri, and others. Six versions have been published so far.

7. Padamawat. Epic composed in 1540 by the famous Muslim poet Malik Muhammad Jayasi, superimposing history, legend, and secrets of the kundalini, one on top of the other, in Avadhi (form of medieval Hindi still spoken widely in the eastern part of the Uttar Pradesh state of India).

8. The continuity of such conviviance would have prevented what is now erroneously termed the "conflict of civilizations."

9. Two major divisions of monastic orders in India.

10. Madarsa and maqtab, Islamic schools and colleges.

11. Just as the names of Greek philosophers are mispronounced by English speakers, they are also mispronounced by Islamic scholars. Socrates is Sukraat, Plato is Aflatoon, Aristotle is Arastu. One does not come across an Aristotle Restaurant in the West, but on a recent trip to Hyderabad, near the famous Muslim monument Chaar Meenaar, was seen a big Arastu Restaurant. Such is the regard for the Greek philosophers among the Islamic philosophers and lay people alike.

12. Gerots. They recite the epics, village lore, and genealogies. It is from these that Alex Haley (1976), author of *Roots,* heard the stories of the enslavement perpetrated by the slave traders.

13. See Arya (1968).

14. If the reader has no access to a Master School, the *Karate Kid* movie series may be watched.

15. Kalari. The system of martial arts taught and practiced in the Kerala state of India. It may be assumed that Bodhidharma, the founder of the ShaoLin monastery, a Brahmin from Kerala, may have included his kalari heritage in developing the Chinese martial arts.

16. Manipuri. The system of martial arts taught and practiced in the Manipur state in far Eastern India.

17. Akhada. The exercise grounds and training institutions for body-building and related traditional arts such as the Indian system of massage and wrestling. They are common in northern India in the villages and

towns. These are run by ustads (master trainers).

18. The ancient founder of Ayurvedic surgery. His Sanskrit text is entitled *Sushruta-samhita*.

19. *Charaka-samhita*. The most ancient and authentic text of the philosophy and application of the Indian system of medical science.

20. The last of these was sacked in 11th century A.D. by fundamentalist and fanatic foreign invaders whose descendants have recently demolished the Buddha at Bamiyan. Monks and students were massacred and the library, it is said, smoldered for six months.

21. Examples: (1) Nepi day, an annual day of silence, is a Balinese Hindu tradition observed by the wider (98 percent Muslim) population of Indonesia; (2) the Nordic "pagan" festival of the worship of Odin and Thor incorporated into Christianity as "Christmas;" (3) "Christian" Christmas and Western New Year (from the 1st of January) are celebrated worldwide; (4) Ramzan fast kept by many Hindus; (5) Use of kava by Hindus in Fiji, and many others.

22. The spiritual guides who know these sacramental practices still exist and may be found.

23. Read works of Gandhi and Aldous Huxley's (1969) *Ends and Means*.

24. In Thailand, the youths, including the royal princes, are often sent to a Buddhist Monastery to live like monks for about three months at some point in their education.

Chapter 9:

1. The first Hindu lawgiver, whose code is still followed in Hindu law, now with many modifications.

2. The commentary on the laws of Yajnavalkya (1924), another ancient Hindu lawgiver; the detailed rules of legal conduct laid down in Mitakshara are followed by the courts to this day.

3. The "five beloved ones" to whom the last guru of the Sikhs, after testing their commitment to self-sacrifice, passed on the right for the continuity of the faith. To this day, it is a privilege to be chosen as the "panj piyare" for any special ceremonies, processions, and major Sikh events.

4. The Indian system of village administration as well as mediation.

Five heads of the village, or any society or community, are elected to carry on the administration. In the case of a dispute, each party may nominate two such judges from their side, with the fifth one to be agreed to by both parties, or in the absence of such agreement, to be selected/elected by the four. The word of the Panch, "the five," is binding on all.

5. The Sikh temples where the Guru Granth Sahib (Veda Bharati, 1998) ("Holy Book as the Guru") is enshrined. The literal meaning of "guru-dwara" is the "guru's door" or the "door to guru's house.

References

Ali, M. (1995). Holy Qur'an. Columbus, OH: Ahmadiyyah Anjuman Isha'at Islam Lahore.

Alter, R. (2011). The wisdom books: Job, proverbs, and Ecclesiastes. New York: W. W. Norton.

Arya, U. (1968). Ritual songs and folk songs of the Hindus of Surinam. Leiden, Netherlands: E. J. Brill.

Arya, U. (1979). God. Honesdale, PA: Himalayan Press.

Atharvaveda samhita (1986). Gurukula Jhajjara, India: Harayana Sahitya Samsthana.

Baker, A. & McCann, J. (1952). The cloud of unknowing, and other treatises. Westminster, MD: Newman Press.

Band, A. (1978). Nahman of Bratislav: The tales. New York: Paulist Press.

Buber, M. & Marx, O. (1947). Tales of the Hasidim. New York: Schocken Books.

Buck, W. (1976). Ramayana. New York: New American Library.

Buhler, G. (1964). Sacred books of the East series, volume 25. New Delhi, India: Motilal Banarsidass Publishers.

Byrom, T. (1990). The heart of awareness: A translation of the Ashtavakra gita. Boston: Shambhala.

Cadet, J. (1971). The Ramakien: The Thai epic. Tokyo: Kodansha.

Carter, J. & Palihawadana, M. (1998). The Dhammapada. New York: Oxford University Press.

Charing, D. (1993). The Torah. Oxford: Heinemann.

Christensen, J. (1958). The role of proverbs in Fante culture. Africa: Journal of the International African Institute. Cambridge, MA: Cambridge University Press.

Dan, J. (2005). Jewish thought and philosophy. In L. Jones, M. Eliade, & C. Adams (Eds.), Encyclopedia of religion. Detroit, MI: Macmillan Reference USA.

Detroit News (2003). Church takes fiery stance on witchcraft. August 7.

Dharasvami. (1983). Shri vyasamaharshiproktam shrimad-bhagavata-puranam. Delhi, India: Motilal Banarsidass.

Doniger, W. (1991). The laws of manu. London: Penguin Books.

Ekadasopanisadah (1966). Delhi, India: Motilal Banarasidass.

Encyclopaedia Britannica Science Supplement (1973).

Fairbanks, A. (1898). Zeno commentary. In A. Fairbanks (Ed.), The first philosophers of Greece. London: K. Paul, Trench, & Trubner. pp. 112-118.

Faiss, K. & Humbach, H. (2010). Zarathushtra and his antagonists: A sociolinguistic study with English and German translations of his Gathas. Wiesbaden, Germany: Reichart Verlag.

Feng, G. & English, J. (1972). Tao te ching. New York: Vintage Books.

Franck, A. (1940). The Kabbalah: The religious philosophy of the Hebrews. New York: Bell Publishing Company.

Gambhirananda, S. (1983). Brahma Sutra bhasya of Shankaracharya. Calcutta, India: Advaita Ashrama.

Ganss, G. (1991). Ignatius of Loyola: The spiritual exercises and selected works. New York: Paulist Press.

Geldner, K. (1986). Avesta. Stuttgart, Germany: Kohlhammer.

Haley, A. (1976). Roots. Garden City, NY: Doubleday.

Hammer, R. (1995). The classic Midrash: Tannaitic commentaries on the Bible. Ramsey, NJ: Paulist Press.

Hariharananda Aranya, S. (1983). Yoga philosophy of Patanjali. Albany, NY: State University of New York.

Holy Bible: The New King James Version (1982). Nashville, TN: T. Nelson.

Hume, R. (1971). The thirteen principal Upanishads. London: Oxford University Press.

Huxley, A. (1969). Ends and means. London: Chatto & Windus.

Huxley, A. (1970). The perennial philosophy. New York: Harper and Row.

International Herald Tribune (2000). September 8, 2.

Jewish Virtual Library (2008). The virtual Jewish history tour—India. American-Israeli Cooperative Enterprise. http://www.jewishvirtuallibrary.org/jsource/Judaism/indians.html.

Johnson, B. & Sakkariya (2004). Selections and notes; Oh, lovely parrot!: Jewish women's songs from kerala. Jerusalem, Israel: Jewish Music

Research Center, Hebrew University of Jerusalem.

Jung, C. (1981). The archetypes and the collective unconscious. In Collected works of C. G. Jung, volume 9, number 1. Princeton, NJ: Princeton University Press.

Kamali, M. (2008). Shari'ah law: An introduction. Oxford: Oneworld.

Kane, P. (1941). History of dharmashastra: Ancient and mediaeval religions and civil law in India, volume 2, chapter 33. Poona, India: Bhandarkar Oriental Research Institute.

Kaplan, A. (1978). Meditation and the Bible. New York: Samuel Weiser.

Kaplan, A. (1982). Meditation and kabbalah. York Beach, ME: Samuel Weiser.

Kaplan, A. (1985). Jewish meditation: A practical guide. New York: Schocken Books.

Kashyap, R. (2003). Rig veda mantra samhita. Bangalore, India: Sri Aurobindu Kapali Sastry Institute of Vedic Studies.

Katz, N. (1994). Jewish-hindu dialogue. Hinduism today, July. Gainesville, FL: University of Florida, Department of Religious Studies.

Katz, N. & Herzog, A. (2007). India. In Skolnik, F. (Ed.), Encyclopaedia Judaica. Detroit, MI: Macmillan Reference USA.

Keith, A. (2008). The Yajur veda: Taittiriya Sanhita. Forgotten Books.

Kunhikrishnan, K. (2003). Literary review of "Indian Jews and their heritage." The Hindu, September, 7.

Lutz, A., Greischar, L., Rawlings, N., Ricard, M., & Davidson, R. (2004). Long-term meditators self-induce high amplitude gamma synchrony during mental practice. Proceedings of the National Academy of Sciences, 101(46), 16369-16373.

Macdonell, A., Muller, F., & Oldenberg, H. (2005). The golden book of the Holy Vedas. Delhi, India: Vijay Goel.

Malhotra, K. (2007). Sacred groves in India: An overview. Bhopal, India: Indira Gandhi Rashtriya Manav Sangrahalaya.

Malik M. & Mataprasada G. (1963). Padmavata. Allahabad, India: Bharati Bhandara.

Mandela, N. (1994). Long walk to freedom: The autobiography of

Nelson Mandela. Boston: Little/Brown.

Maududi, A. (1996). Quran. Delhi, India: Islami Sahitya Prakashan.

Mbiti, J. (1969). African religions and philosophy. New York: Praeger.

Mishra, R. (2002). A spotlight on Mitakshara school. Orissa, India: The Law House.

Mueller, M. (1984). The Iliad. London: Allen & Unwin.

Narasimhan, C. (1965). The Mahabharata. New York: Columbia University Press.

Nelson, L. (1998). Purifying the earthly body of God: Religion and ecology in Hindu India. Albany, NY: State University of New York Press.

Neusner, J. (1991). The Mishnah: A new translation. New Haven, CT: Yale University Press.

Nicodemus (1979). In Palmer, G., Sherrard, P., & Kallistos, T. (Eds.), The Philokalia: The complete text. London: Faber and Faber.

Ovid (1986). Metamorphoses. Oxford: Oxford University Press.

Panikkar, R. (1977). The Vedic experience: Mantramanjari. Berkeley, CA: University of California Press.

Pullman, P. (2005). Paradise lost. Oxford, England: Oxford University.

Qu, Y. & Field, S. (1986). Tian wen: A chinese book of origins. New York: New Directions.

Radhakrishnan, S. (1948). The Bhagavadgita. New York: Harper & Brothers.

Rama, S. (1988). Enlightenment without God. Honesdale, PA: Himalayan Institute Press.

Ramos, J. (2000). The five virtues of Kofi Annan. Time, September 4, 156, 10, 34.

Ranjan, N. (2008). Vishvarupa: Paintings on the cosmic form of krishna-vasudeva. New Delhi, India: Arya Books International.

Recinos, A., Goetz, D., & Morley, S. (1965). Popul Vuh: The sacred book of the ancient quiche maya. New York: Simon and Schuster.

Sandars, N. (1972). The epic of Gilgamesh: An English version with an introduction. Harmondsworth, England: Penguin Books.

Santoso, S. (1975). Sutasoma: A study in old Javanese vajrayana. New Delhi, India: International Academy of Indian Culture. p. 578.

Shankaracarya (1977). Bhagavad gita. Madras, India: Samata.

Sharma, P. (2004). Charaka samhita. Varanasi, India: Chaukhambha Orientalia.

Shirreff, A. (1944). Padmavati of Malik Muhammad Jaisi. Mumbai, India: The Asiatic Society.

Simon, M. (1984). The Zohar, volumes 1-5. Brooklyn, NY: Soncino Press.

Singh, J. (1989). Shri guru granth sahib: Hindi shabdartha. Patiyala: Publication Bureau, Panjabi University.

Singh, M. (1970). Lorikayana: Haradi gariha ki lariai. Varanasi, India: Thakuraprasada.

Skolnik, F. (Ed.), (2007). Encyclopaedia Judaica. Detroit, MI: Macmillan Reference.

Srikantan, K. (2007). Administration of justice in ancient India. Mumbai, India: Bharatiya Vidya Bhavan.

Sushruta, D. & Sharma, P. (1999). Sushruta-samhita. Varanasi, India: Chaukhambha Vishvabharati.

Time (2000), September 4.

Times of India (2000). October 9.

Times of India (2001). February 12, 9.

Times of India (2009a). September 8.

Times of India (2009b). September Roza.

Tolstoy, L. (2011). The kingdom of God is within you. Los Angeles: CreateSpace Independent Publishing.

Uvvata, M. & Sharma, R. (1912). Shuklayajurvedasamhita. Benares City, India: Chowkhamba Sanskrit Book Depot.

Vail, S. (2002). India's Jewish heritage: Ritual, art and life-cycle. Mumbai, India: Marg Publications.

van Buitenen, J. (1996). The archaism of the Bhagavata Purana. In S. Shashi (Ed.), Encyclopedia Indica. New Delhi, India: Anmol Publications. pp. 28–45.

Veda Bharati, S. (1997). Special mantras. Rishikesh, India: Swami Rama Sadhaka Grama Publications.

Veda Bharati, S. (1998). Introduction to Guru granth sahib. Dehradun, India: Himalayan Institute Hospital Trust, Swami Ram Nagar.

Veda Bharati, S. (1999). Perennial in the millennium. Minneapolis,

MN: The Meditation Center.

Veda Bharati, S. (2000). Yoga: Polity, economy, and family. In Night Birds. Rishikesh, India: Swami Rama Sadhaka Grama Publications. pp. 185-205.

Veda Bharati, S. (2001). Yoga sutras of Patanjali, volume II. New Delhi, India: Motilal Banarsidass Publishers.

Veda Bharati, S. (2002a). Subtler than the subtle: The Upanishad of the White Horse. Saint Paul, MN: Yes International Publishers.

Veda Bharati, S. (2002b). Bhishma: Introducing Mahabharata. Rishikesh, India: Swami Rama Sadhaka Grama Publications.

Verber, E. (1990). Talmud. Beograd, Serbia: BIGZ.

Weil, S. (Ed.) (2002). India's Jewish heritage. Mumbai, India: Marg Publications.

Werblowsky, R. (1995). Transmigration. In L. Jones, M. Eliade, & C. Adams, (Eds.), Encyclopedia of religion. Detroit, MI: Macmillan Reference USA.

Yajnavalkya (1924). Yajnavalkya-smriti. Benares, India: Chowkhamba Sanskrit Series Office.

Young, J. (2005). Schopenhauer. New York: Routledge.

Swami Veda Bharati, D.Litt. Association of Himalayan Yoga Meditation Societies International; www.swamiveda.org; ahymsin@gmail.com; info@themeditationcenter.org

For a complete list of books, audio cassettes, CDs, and more, please contact: Ahymsin Publishers, Swami Rama Sadhaka Grama, Virpur Khurd, Virbhadra Road, Rishikesh, 249203 (Uttarakhand), India. Phone: 91-135-245-3030, 245-3440; email: ahymsinpublishers@gmail.com, or The Meditation Center, 631 University Avenue, N.E., Minneapolis, MN 55413; phone: 612-379-2386; email: info@themeditationcenter.org.

For more information on Swami Veda Bharati and his activities, please see: www.themeditationcenter.org, www.swamiveda.org, or email him directly at ahymsin@gmail.com.